Othello

Fenella Salgādo, who is Deputy Head of Ercall Wood School, Wellington, has taught in Uganda, Scotland, Ireland and England. She holds an M.A. in American Studies from Sussex University and an Honours degree in English from Queen's University, Belfast, where one of her tutors was Gāmini Salgādo, who had also taught at the universities of Singapore and Sussex, and at Earlham College, Indiana, before becoming Professor of English at the University of Exeter.

Gāmini Salgādo's books include *Eyewitnesses of Shakespeare, The Elizabethan Underworld, A Preface to Lawrence* and *English Drama: A Critical Introduction.* He edited *Three Jacobean Tragedies, Three Restoration Comedies, Four Jacobean City Comedies* and *Cony-Catchers and Bawdy Baskets* for the Penguin Classics.

His other publications include *King Lear: Text and Performance, The Everyman Companion to the Theatre* (written with Professor Peter Thomas of Exeter) and *The Spirit of D. H. Lawrence,* which he edited with Professor G. K. Das of Delhi University. Professor Salgādo died in June 1985.

Penguin Critical Studies
Advisory Editors:
Stephen Coote and Bryan Loughrey

Shakespeare

Othello

Fenella and Gāmini Salgādo

Penguin Books

PENGUIN BOOKS

Published by the Penguin Group
27 Wrights Lane, London W8 5TZ, England
Viking Penguin Inc., 40 West 23rd Street, New York, New York 10010, USA
Penguin Books Australia Ltd, Ringwood, Victoria, Australia
Penguin Books Canada Ltd, 2801 John Street, Markham, Ontario, Canada L3R 1B4
Penguin Books (NZ) Ltd, 182–190 Wairau Road, Auckland 10, New Zealand

Penguin Books Ltd, Registered Offices: Harmondsworth, Middlesex, England

First published 1985
10 9 8 7 6 5 4

Copyright © Fenella and Gāmini Salgādo, 1985
All rights reserved

Made and printed in Great Britain by
Richard Clay Ltd, Bungay, Suffolk
Filmset in 9/11 pt Monophoto Times

To David
For his eighteenth birthday

Contents

Introduction

Since *Othello* is a play, it could be argued that there is something artificial about reading and studying it as a text. A play unfolds in time, at a tempo which the director or actor has determined, and a line once spoken or a scene once over can never be brought back, at least not in the same performance. A play text, on the other hand, can be read at whatever pace the reader finds most convenient, with as many returns to individual lines or scenes as necessary. These two experiences are quite different, though there are some important areas of overlap between them. In the case of a Shakespeare play, one crucial connection is that some of the most important *dramatic* effects are achieved not by spectacular scenery or striking changes of lighting or music (the first two were absent in the original Shakespearean stage and the third sparingly used), but by the use of *language*. In watching a Shakespeare play, we may not be aware of *how* the language affects us, but only *that* it affects us; in reading, we have the opportunity to consider how some of these effects are achieved. Unless we were moved by the dramatic experience of *Othello*, we would scarcely bother to analyse that experience. But if the experience does affect us, we may be interested in the means used by the dramatist to reach our hearts and minds. We have therefore tried to treat *Othello* as a drama whose essential life is on the stage, but one in which language plays a crucial part. To this end we have followed the sequence of the play scene by scene as it unfolds before us, using the text as a kind of score which, as it were, encapsulates the performance. We have tried to take note of such matters as character, theme and imagery in relation to specific dramatic situations rather than as abstractions. Having done this, we have gone on to discuss briefly some of the major issues that arise in the play. An annotated list of suggestions for further reading concludes the essay.

Part One: The play

Act I, Scene 1

Shakespeare was, among many other things, a master of the dramatic opening scene, but in few of his plays does he succeed so brilliantly in creating tension and mystery and suggesting relationships in the very first lines. As often, we are pitched into the middle of a conversation, and a somewhat heated one at that. The speaker is evidently aggrieved at some sort of betrayal of trust, apparently concerned with money, though we are as yet in the dark as to what 'this' is. It is difficult to attend to the words of a play as well known as *Othello* as if we were hearing them for the first time, but if we make the effort we realize the mastery with which the dramatist creates and heightens our interest. So far we hear the nameless voices, one complaining, the other placatory, talking of money and a third person whom one of the speakers claims to hate. As we listen to Iago, we may be struck by the readiness with which he resorts to oaths: ' 'Sblood!', 'Abhor me', 'Despise me' and the like. This is perhaps natural in a professional soldier, but it also serves to indicate the assertive nature of the man and his sense that what Roderigo needs most of all is assurance. This is what Iago continues to give him in every scene in which they meet until their final fatal encounter. We are no wiser when whatever Roderigo refers to as 'this' becomes 'such a matter' to Iago, and while his ensuing speech gives a clear account of a particular incident, we do not yet know who the 'him' is who figures in the episode. It is not till some thirty lines later that we discover the exact relationship between Iago and the unnamed 'him' – that of officer and subordinate – and the alleged source of his grievance – that he has been passed over for promotion. But, as usual with Shakespeare, the speech does far more than engage with the fundamentals of the plot. It tells us, in the first place, a good deal about the speaker's opinion of himself: 'I know my price, I am worth no worse a place'. We shall discover, as we become more involved with the fast-moving action, that this sense of injured merit is as important an element in Iago's character as it is in that of Milton's Satan. Secondly, he attributes to his unnamed superior self love and overweening self-confidence ('as loving his own pride and purposes') as the motive for rejecting him, Iago. Thirdly, his scorn of Michael Cassio for being a mere 'arithmetician' (that is, a theorist only) reveals the experienced soldier's dismissal of 'bookish theoric' and abstract ideas. And finally, it shows Iago as a representative of the traditional virtues of loyalty and devoted professionalism, undeservedly neglected due to the corruption of the times. We may notice the irony that Iago begins by complaining that the influence of 'three great ones of the city' was insufficient to win his suit, and ends by complaining that 'preferment goes by letter and affection'. Now at last we gain another vital piece of information about his superior officer – that he is a Moor – though how vital this is we do not yet realize.

Though we cannot yet say whether Iago is justified in his complaint or not, we already feel the confidence, energy and dry wit which we shall respond to as key elements in his personality, as well as the subtle blend of buttonholing intimacy and no-nonsense manliness with which he flatters Roderigo. The rhythm of his lines is in strong contrast to the petulant whining of Roderigo, and the sardonic humour of lines like 'A fellow almost damned in a fair wife' or 'And I – God bless the mark! – his moorship's ancient' is immediately attractive. This is clearly a man whose fortunes would be worth following.

As he continues, however, the tone and implications of his speech become darker and more menacing. 'O sir, content you' he tells Roderigo, and the phrase bespeaks one who knows exactly what he is about, 'I follow him to serve my turn upon him' and, more chillingly,

> *We cannot all be masters, nor all masters*
> *Cannot be truly followed.*

There follow little cameos of two kinds of follower, of which the speaker claims to belong to the second, those who 'keep yet their hearts attending on themselves'. We may wonder why one who professes to be such a cunning villain should be so candid in revealing his own nature. In part this is due to a dramatic convention which Shakespeare inherited from the medieval drama, that of the self-defining villain who takes the audience into his confidence, as Richard III does in his opening soliloquy. But Shakespeare rarely used a convention lazily or inertly, nor should we be satisfied to explain anything in his plays as merely a convention. Here there are at least two other reasons for Iago's candour. One is that, as we are already beginning to suspect, Roderigo is such a fool that Iago can safely tell him the truth, or part of it. Indeed, he is the only one of the characters to whom Iago does speak frankly, confident that he will not be believed. The other and more important reason is that Iago, for all his self-confidence and apparent self-sufficiency, needs an audience. Someone has to appreciate the virtuosity of his villainy, and Roderigo is plainly a very poor judge: this is why at the earliest opportunity Iago makes it clear that the audience to whom he looks for genuine appreciation of his skill and resourcefulness is ourselves. Like some other Shakespearean villains – Richard III, and Edmund in *King Lear*, for example – Iago captivates us with his charm and energy and almost traps us into endorsing his deviousness and treachery. He is an incarnation of the capacity of the theatre to undermine moral values through the amoral ones of style, eloquence and vitality. As the intrigue develops, we need constantly to bear in mind Iago's plainly spoken warning: 'I am not what I am'.

While the uncertainty about the Moor and his treatment of his ensign and the possible connection with Roderigo is still unresolved, a further mystery is added, this time that of an unnamed 'her' whose father has apparently suffered some loss or misfortune. Once again, the familiarity of the play may have dulled our sense of the suspense Shakespeare creates here. The sudden disruption of Brabantio's peace prefigures many similar scenes of violent interruption. It is not until Brabantio has been roused by cries of 'Thieves! thieves!' that the full story emerges; and the terms in which that story is told are deliberately violent and obscenely animalistic:

> *Even now, now, very now, an old black ram*
> *Is tupping your white ewe.*

The theme of racial tension, which is to cast such an enormous shadow over the action, is introduced here in the crudest possible way, linked as it is to the imagery of bestial copulation which we shall learn to identify with Iago's way of looking at the human world. We are far from clear as to what is going on or Iago's motives (though we remember his warning: 'I am not what I am'), but we cannot help admiring the directness and sense of purpose which ring out through his succession of imperatives: 'Awake!', 'Look to your house', 'Put on your gown!' and 'Arise, arise!'

This is the first clear indication we have that the opening scene takes place at night, and on the Jacobean stage where performances took place in daylight it would be the original audience's first indication as well. In a modern production, lighting effects would serve to heighten the general air of tension and uncertainty. Brabantio's answer to Roderigo helps to clarify on the mystery. We now learn that Roderigo has been an unwelcome suitor to the old man's daughter. In Brabantio's initial refusal to be convinced that there is anything amiss we understand what sort of place the action occurs in. 'What tell'st me thou of robbing?' he angrily demands, 'this is Venice:/My house is not a grange'. A grange is an isolated farmhouse, far from the amenities of civilization and order, which Brabantio contrasts with the simple proper name 'Venice'. In its golden days, which included the time when *Othello* was originally performed, Venice was the greatest commercial republic in Europe, a city built on water and on the wealth that came by water, civilized and democratic by the standards of the day, jealously guarding its enormous commercial empire with military strength drawn, where necessary, from mercenary forces. To Brabantio it is inconceivable that robbery and violence could occur in the heart of such a centre of refinement and civil order. Very soon the action is to move from Venice to an outpost of the Venetian commercial empire, Cyprus, where the Venetian writ does not go unchallenged. These two places may well stand for the two poles of the play, its symbolic geography, so to speak. On the one hand we have civility, culture and control and on the other turbulent passion and violent intrigue.

Iago's scornful taunting soon convinces Brabantio, the more easily since he had apparently had a dream prophesying such a disaster. The search is now on for the eloping daughter and her alleged and still unnamed abductor. We gather that the distraught father is a man of consequence in the republic ('I may command at most') and we learn too that war with Cyprus is imminent and that 'the Moor' is vitally important for the military security of Venice. Something of the trust which the Moor reposes in Iago may be inferred from the fact that the latter knows where the couple are staying. Brabantio's distracted utterances are interspersed with a thought that is to recur throughout the early phase of the action, namely that his daughter has been abducted through charms or witchcraft. The theme of witchcraft and unnatural powers and practices will return, tragically transformed, towards the end of the play.

Thus this opening scene has not only created suspense and excitement, but has introduced some important themes and interests – secret love and secret hate, military and domestic threats, racial tension and the contrast between passionate impulse and civilized control – in such a manner that we can hardly help being interested and involved. Furthermore, by centring the dialogue and action almost exclusively on the eloping couple without as yet presenting them to us in person, the dramatist has greatly increased our desire to meet them, especially this mysterious Moor on whom the state relies so heavily and who has, literally or otherwise, charmed the daughter of one of the republic's leading citizens.

Act I, Scene 2

When we at last meet him it is in Iago's company. But this is a very different Iago from the one we have just seen. If we had not had some hint of his real nature and purposes from himself, we would almost certainly consider his opening words to Othello those of an honest, loyal, courageous, impulsive man more used to practical action than elaborate argument – just such a man, in fact, as Iago wants to be thought, and, as we shall see, succeeds in making all Venice take him to be. The half-line Othello speaks in reply to his protestation is eloquent in its brevity. It seems to come from a man who wastes no words but who can make each word resonate with a sense of fixed purpose. Later we see that Othello has a very clear public image of himself but is less sure in the more intimate sphere of domestic life. Iago's anxious inquiries as to his master's present state and misgivings about possible repercussions sound somehow trivial by contrast to Othello's weighty terseness, and in any case we are no longer inclined, if we ever were, to take them at their face value. In Othello's next speech we hear for the first time in its full scope that rich and ample mode of utterance which is unmistakably Othello's throughout the play until it is contaminated by treachery and mistrust. One Shakespearean critic has called this 'the *Othello* music' but it properly belongs not to the play but to Othello himself. It is the richest of the many voices in the play but we should not dull our ears to the others, more devious, more meagre or more pathetic as they may be. The most immediate sign of 'the Othello music' is a certain expansiveness of rhythm, a measured and steady fulness of speech which is felt as much in the many open vowel sounds as in the unfaltering control of syntax. Later, we shall see that it is typically associated with the forces of nature rather than with those of civilization – sea and sky and a vast open landscape of caves, deserts and gigantic mountains. This speech consists of only three sentences, moving from calm rebuttal to dignified statement of purpose. Othello's subsequent torment and downfall can be traced almost as much in the disappearance of these rhetorical qualities as in anything he says or does. The imagery of the sea with which Othello is particularly associated is traditionally symbolic of power, mystery, richness and strangeness.

Watching on stage the entry of officers with torches, we may be forgiven for thinking this is Brabantio and his search party, especially as Iago makes the same mistake. Once again, Othello's response – 'Not I: I must be found' – is one we shall discover to be typical, literally a world away from the bestial lecherousness with which Iago attempted to link him in the earlier scene. Shakespeare panders to our lurking feelings of racial bigotry, and probably to those of his original audience, only to subvert them by showing how manifestly unjust they are in the given case. He does something similar with Shylock in *The Merchant of Venice,* though there the prejudice of the Christians is given more to justify it. In speech, appearance and demeanour, Othello literally towers above those around him, as he does above those in the second search party which arrives very shortly. The two search parties represent on stage the mingling of the public political action caused by the Turkish threat of Cyprus with the domestic and private crisis of Othello's marriage which gives this tragedy its distinctive atmosphere. Somewhat misleadingly, *Othello* has been called a domestic tragedy, which it is not, if we take a play like Ibsen's *Ghosts* to be a representative domestic tragedy. But compared with the other great tragedies, the political range of *Othello* is limited both in scope and duration.

The fact that no fewer than three urgent messages have been sent from the Duke and Council to Othello underlies his key position in the security of Venice. In the light of what we learn later, Cassio's ignorance of Othello's wedding is somewhat strange, but he may simply wish not to let Iago see how much he knows for fear of betraying Othello's confidence. The suspense is increased by the arrival of Brabantio's party just when Othello is ready to leave. There is an immediate and striking contrast between the way Brabantio addresses Othello – 'Down with him, thief!' – and the massive dignity of the Moor's response:

> *Keep up your bright swords, for the dew will rust them.*

Perhaps no single line he speaks in the play is so full of 'the Othello music'. Three times in his long speech of accusation Brabantio repeats the charge of witchcraft against Othello, who does not deign to reply but calmly agrees to accompany his accusers, merely pointing out that he is already wanted at the Signiory on state business of urgency. Thus the public and private themes are interwoven both in speech and dramatic action. Before we leave this scene, we may note Iago's 'courageous' challenge to Roderigo cunningly enhancing the image of the honest, brave and loyal soldier.

Act I, Scene 3

Before Othello, Brabantio and the rest arrive at the Signiory, we have a brief discussion between the Duke and his councillors about the military situation. The chief impression we gain from this (and it is one which is vital to the concerns of the tragedy as a whole) is that the various items of news relating to the war are inconsistent with each other and that the Turks may be deliberately trying to mislead the Venetians by their tactics:

> 'Tis a pageant
> To keep us in false gaze.

This problem of evaluating different and contradictory pieces of information, and the difficulty of distinguishing between a false front deliberately adopted and the reality behind it, is one that faces not only most of the major characters in the play but ourselves as readers or audience. How many of us, for instance, would be able to see through Iago without the help he so obligingly gives us by self-description? And how soon?

With the arrival of Othello and his accusers, the threat to the security of the state, imminent as it is, is rapidly displaced as the centre of discussion by Brabantio's charge, though it continues to tick away disturbingly at the back of our minds. After the two short scenes with their atmosphere of confusion, suspense and urgency, this one with its longer and more declamatory speeches is somewhat more expansive and is, almost literally, a court-room scene. As such, it sets the pattern for many similar scenes in the play in which a character is accused and judged, often on partial or misleading evidence. Such scenes reach their tragic climax at the very end of the play where the hero becomes accuser, judge, criminal and executioner in turn. Brabantio, explaining his present business, falls naturally into the metaphor of violent floods to express turbulent emotions, a metaphor which will be actualized in the storm through which both Othello and Desdemona pass to reach Cyprus. For the fifth time Brabantio returns to the charge of witchcraft against Othello. To many of the original audience the link between a black man and the devil would have been a powerful if not fully conscious one. In the power and dignity of Othello's answer we have another example of Shakespeare's subversion of the audience's ingrained attitudes and ideas. This speech also helps to create a sense of Othello as a mysterious and powerful stranger who seems rightly to belong to a vaster arena than the civilized, wealthy, secure and respectable city state in which he now finds himself. We need not take too literally his protestation that he lacks eloquence, since he belies it every time he opens his mouth. It is perhaps Othello's version of 'Unaccustomed as I am to public speaking ...' With deliberate emphasis he addresses himself to the specific charge brought against him:

> *I will a round unvarnished tale deliver*
> *Of my whole course of love: what drugs, what charms,*
> *What conjuration and what mighty magic –*
> *For such proceedings am I charged withal –*
> *I won his daughter.*

Brabantio repeats the charge, whereupon Othello asks that Desdemona herself should be summoned to testify. While she is sent for (once more heightening our expectancy) Othello speaks not only of his present situation but of the fate and fortune which has brought him to it. Since a dramatic character 'lives' only during the brief duration of his existence on stage, this kind of retrospective account, whether offered by himself or others, is an important way of giving the character depth and solidity. The contrast between the variety and amplitude of Othello's experience and the cosy limits of the tight little money-making island is crucial to the tragedy. It gives point and meaning to the earlier lines where Othello assures Iago that nothing but his love for Desdemona would have induced him to give up the soldier's life. In one sense the seeds of the tragedy are there, in the abandonment by a brave professional soldier of the only life he knows, that of the tented field, for the unknown perils of love and marriage in one of Europe's most sophisticated societies.

We learn that Othello was Desdemona's father's friend, which gives us a clue to his age, which is to seem significant later. We learn, too, that it is Desdemona who takes the initiative in placing the tales of heroic adventure in the context of possible matrimony:

> *She thanked me,*
> *And bade me, if I had a friend that loved her,*
> *I should but teach him how to tell my story,*
> *And that would woo her.*

Thus, as with Othello himself, we are presented with conflicting views of Desdemona; on the one hand that of 'a maiden never bold', on the other of a girl bold enough to initiate a courtship and resolute enough to pursue it to the point of elopement. Not surprisingly we await her arrival with eagerness. Before we hear her speak we note the Duke's acknowledgement of the power of Othello's tale and may wonder uneasily whether such rhetorical 'charm' is an adequate basis for a lasting adult relationship. We should also observe that Brabantio, for all his earlier confident assurance, seems to consider the possibility that his daughter was 'half the wooer'. Perhaps this links up with the prophetic dream he has had and it may have its basis in an unacknowledged guilt that he has failed in his duty as a father. Certainly as Desdemona's speech continues we realize that the father has grotesquely misunderstood his daughter's true nature. Listening to the clear, unsentimental and calmly confident accents of Desdemona, how can we possibly assent to such a description of her as this?

> *A maiden never bold;*
> *Of spirit so still and quiet that her motion*
> *Blushed at herself; ...*

Brabantio's misjudgement of his daughter is one of many instances in the play of bad judgement based on appearances and even more on what the person judging *wants* to be the truth, for the sake of his own self-image and psychological security. Desdemona's defence recalls in both word and spirit that of Cordelia in *King Lear* when she defends herself against *her* father's imperious and overbearing demand for total love. It also gives indirectly an instance where judgement is explicitly *not* based on outward appearance: 'I saw Othello's visage in his mind'. There is a kind of irony in the fact that while Desdemona sees her marriage as a total commitment of herself to Othello's martial life, 'My heart's subdued/Even to the very quality of my lord', Othello has already told us that his marriage signifies at least a partial forsaking of the soldierly life. The explosive potentialities of this incongruity are not kept below the surface very long.

The dignity and finality of Brabantio's acceptance of his loss contrast sharply with the Duke's clumsy effort to offer general comfort as a balm for particular pain. The platitudinous emptiness of his words is underlined by the banal rhyming couplets which are bitterly parodied and rejected in Brabantio's rejoinder:

> *But words are words; I never yet did hear*
> *That the bruised heart was piecèd through the ear.*

We may be slightly taken aback by the readiness with which Othello accepts his military duties, but we should bear in mind that his position in Venice as one who is 'all in all sufficient' depends on his absolute professional competence and reliability. The Duke's attempts to reconcile the parties by having Desdemona stay with her father are of a piece with his ham-fisted words of comfort and are roundly rejected by all concerned. So little is Desdemona like her father's description of her that she is not afraid to refer openly to her conjugal dues: 'The rites for which I love him'. Othello's disclaimer that it is not mere sensual appetite which leads him to support his bride's request to accompany him is somewhat puzzling. He may be saying that he no longer has the clamorous sexual needs of a young man. He is certainly confident that the demands of love-making will in no way be allowed to interfere with those of duty. The very assertiveness with which he makes this claim recalls Brabantio's earlier confidence about his daughter and may once more raise a doubt in our minds as to how deep Othello's love goes. Desdemona has just spoken out clearly and freely in defence of *her* love, but her newly wedded husband seems to be willing and able to put it aside a shade too easily. Is it reading too much into his lines about heat and defunct appetites to find in them a deep-seated fear of physical sexuality? The very fact that the question can arise is yet further evidence of Shakespeare undermining the stereotype of 'the black man' as an incarnation of gross physical sexuality, as he undermines the other principal components of that stereotype, cruelty and ugliness.

The atmosphere of haste and danger never slackens till the decision is made that Othello should sail immediately for Cyprus. We find here the first of many testimonials to the 'public' character of Iago, one which he has so painstakingly built up for his own purposes: 'A man he is of honesty and trust'. In the light of later events, we should not be too hasty to convict Othello of excessive credulity, for we discover that virtually everyone in Venice has the same high view of Iago's reliability and straightforwardness. Whatever else it may be, *Othello* is not a tragedy about a credulous fool. Rather it is about the perilously shaky foundations of prejudice, self-esteem and self-interest on which our judgements of others are often based. From this standpoint, Othello himself is not very different from many in Venice and, no doubt, in the audience.

The Duke's parting words to Brabantio, kindly meant as they are, introduce in a gentler key the note of racial difference so brutally sounded earlier by Iago, and at a crucial moment Othello will half-consciously recall Brabantio's ominous warning: 'She has deceived her father, and may thee'.

After the tension and clamour of the public 'examination' of Othello, the act ends on a more subdued note with a discussion between Roderigo and 'honest Iago'. The change to prose helps to lower the emotional temperature and Iago's bantering wit once more engages us. But we shall miss its full impact if we ignore the premises on which it is founded. Iago is wholly serious in his view that a man's chief guiding principle in life ought to be 'to love himself'. The high place he gives to will and choice in the metaphor of the garden and the gardener may in isolation seem to be a defence of free will and self-responsibility, but is in fact an attempt to justify conduct unrelated to any principle except that of ruthless self-advancement. For all the talk of 'motiveless malignity' and the consequent mystery with which Iago has been surrounded, he is a very simple and very limited character, much simpler for instance than Edmund in *King Lear* with whom, as noted earlier, he has some kinship. Iago is thoroughly convinced that he has discovered the master secret which makes him superior to everyone else, namely that he understands the real springs of human action – desire for security and power over others – and is prepared to exploit those less clear-sighted than himself. The play as a whole not only invites but encourages us to question the universal validity of this assumption, and the only way Iago can safeguard it is by consigning all those who appear to be exceptions to his rule to the category of fools.

The vigorous prose which is characteristic of Iago not only betokens his confident egoism but also his tendency to reduce everything to the barest physical and material terms. Love is merely 'a lust of the blood and a permission of the will'. The noble passion of Othello and Desdemona is no more than a squalid affair between 'an erring barbarian and a super-subtle Venetian', based on nothing more lasting or valuable than an old black man's lust for a young white girl and, on her part, a bored sophisticate's perverse yearning for exotic thrills. Above all, the solution to every problem is to 'put money in thy purse' (as a character in Stoppard's *Jumpers* is said to believe that any problem can be solved provided you have a large enough plastic bag). No doubt some of this is intended to convince Roderigo that success with Desdemona is within his reach. But, as noted before, Iago does not have enough respect for Roderigo to bother to deceive him, and the volume and vehemence of his language is sufficient indication that there is genuine conviction, or at least a passionate desire to believe, behind it. In fact, as 'the Othello music' is marked by sweeping rhythms and a sense of absolute values for which elemental forces and precious gems become symbols, so 'the Iago music' is immediately recognizable by its energetic but jangling demotic rhythms, its colloquial turns of phrase, often vaguely obscene in their reference, and its general worm's eye view of human life and passion. We should not fall into the trap Iago sets, for us as much as for Roderigo, of believing that his view of things is somehow closer to objective reality than that of the other characters. Insofar as our perception of reality is inevitably coloured by our temperament, interests and experience, Iago's perception is no more exempt than anyone else's. His is the cynical logic of the commonplace, and of the marketplace too. That his outlook is heavily charged with passion and self-interest is clear from the fulness and assertiveness with which it is expressed. We cannot miss the personal urgency behind his conviction that Desdemona 'must change for youth when she is sated with his body' even without the frenzied repetition that occurs in the Folio text only: 'she must have change, she must'. And in the final soliloquy at the end of this act, he takes us into his confidence and makes the mainspring of his actions perfectly plain. But perhaps he reveals more of himself here than he wishes to. The first thing he wants us to understand is that he associates with a dolt like Roderigo for his own particular purposes and not because he feels any affinity with the young man; he is more than a cut above 'such a snipe' and the whole world must know it. Secondly, he frankly declares 'I hate the Moor' and it is noteworthy that he avows his hate not only before he gives us any reason for it, but as if feeling and its cause were unrelated; the alleged reason is introduced not, as we might have expected, by 'because' but by 'and'. As if to underline his indifference to genuine motives, he then goes on to declare that he will have his revenge on the Moor regardless of whether the reason he has given is true or not. This tells us, not that he has no motive, but that we must look for his true motive deeper than his own declaration. Already it is becoming clear that the need to think of himself as more powerful, more clear-sighted and more resourceful than those about him is this man's ruling passion. No doubt there is a class dimension to this feeling. Iago has to make his way in a highly stratified society without benefit of rank, wealth or birth. The man on the make would have been a familiar figure to the Jacobean audience, with its keen awareness of social gradations.

Finally, we learn from this soliloquy that Iago has a great talent for spotting the weaknesses of others – easy enough to do if one is resolved to see anything other than the narrowest self-regard as weakness – and an even greater talent for thinking on his feet. In this too he resembles Richard III. One of the fascinations of Iago as a dramatic character is the insight he gives us into the workings of his mind in motion; we see his plans in the process of solidifying into action. But for all that, his attitude and language are no more 'objective' than those of anyone else in the play.

Act II, Scene 1

The action now shifts to Cyprus, where it will remain for the rest of the play. The dramatic importance of the contrast between Venice and Cyprus has already been mentioned. We have seen that the world of the first act is one of high civilization and great wealth, the heart of a rich and powerful commercial empire protected by highly paid and well respected military officers and governed by well understood codes of discipline and conduct. It is at the very centre of European culture and its watchwords are order and control. By contrast, Cyprus is in the hinterland of the Venetian empire, a place of danger and uncertainty, yet a key point in Venetian security. Our first introduction to it links Cyprus with the storm raging around its shores, a symbol of impulse and passion, perhaps of ungovernable passion, to set in our minds against the settled rule of Venice. The opening lines, not so much describing as recreating the storm (as so much background and atmosphere were verbally created on the Jacobean stage), not only heighten our anxiety for the safety of the voyagers from Venice but bring before us the fury of the storm as a figure for tumultuous passions unleashed:

> *The chidden billow seems to pelt the clouds;*
> *The wind-shaked surge, with high and monstrous mane,*
> *Seems to cast water on the burning Bear*
> *And quench the guards of th'ever-fixèd Pole.*

Along with news of the providential destruction of the Turkish fleet (which thereby removes the possible distraction of military action from the story) comes news of Cassio's safe arrival. But anxiety is renewed when we learn that Cassio and Othello were parted in the storm. Montano's words further corroborate Othello's skills as warrior and commander, while Cassio's prayers for the safety of Othello and his bride show his close relationship with them, a relationship which is to have tragic results. In particular, his praise of Desdemona is warm but totally without any spark of envy or criticism, and as we listen to it we feel nothing but Cassio's close attachment to and good wishes for the newly wedded pair. When, on hearing of Iago's arrival, Cassio goes on to pay a further glowing tribute to Desdemona, we cannot help feeling uneasy, not only because Iago's own words about his intentions are still ringing in our minds, but because Cassio's exaggerations draw attention to their own ineffectualness. The one thing we can be certain about regarding natural forces, especially in their destructive aspect, is that they have no 'sense of beauty' and 'omit' nothing that lies in their path. Coming hard on the heels of the mention of Iago, Cassio's confidence in Desdemona's safety only increases our sense of her peril, not so much from the blind fury of the storm but rather from the conscious malice of a force almost as great and as wanton in its destructiveness. Cassio's simple and sentimental view

23

of a scheme of things where beauty and virtue are universally honoured is not one which Shakespearean tragedy allows us to maintain for long.

We may feel, as Cassio continues with his praise of Desdemona, that there is perhaps some more intimately personal feeling behind his words: Certainly the lady, whether deliberately or not, brings down the exalted tone of compliment, almost of veneration, in her cool reply, 'I thank you, valiant Cassio', followed by anxious inquiry about her husband. The news of a ship being sighted acts as a kind of marker for our interest while Desdemona and Cassio engage in small talk to fill up the time. Cassio's gallantry towards Emilia is a trifling detail, but it is one of those 'trifles light as air' which Iago is later to make very good or rather very bad use of. Iago's sardonic account of women is partly traditional commonplace expected from the 'honest' character, but here it also strengthens our impression of a man to whom scorn and contempt come more readily than gentler feelings. As he himself declares a little later: 'I am nothing if not critical'. We also begin to discern that this 'critical' spirit of Iago consists in large measure of a habit of abstract generalizing rather than looking at the particularities of an individual character or situation. It is this temper which makes him speak of Othello and Desdemona as 'an erring barbarian and a super-subtle Venetian', deliberately closing his mind to what he knows personally of the individuals concerned. The capacity to make general statements based either on one's own experience of life or on more systematic statistical research is desirable and necessary in many areas such as politics, economics and social studies. But it is grotesquely inappropriate in personal relationships; one does not judge people one knows well in terms of statistical categories. Iago is a social statistician with two vitally important differences; he applies notions of statistical probability to specific individuals disregarding his own personal knowledge of them, and his conclusions are distorted by his passionate prior conviction that they must be right. The bantering exchange between Desdemona and Iago displays in a minor key both his tendency to brutal reductivism and generalization and her firm confidence in a different order of value: 'the authority of ... merit'.

The life-hating viciousness of Iago comes out in his reference to 'clyster-pipes' which in performance is followed immediately by the sound of Othello's trumpet, betokening another world. Othello's words to his new bride soar magnificently to express the pinnacle of his happiness, but even as they do so they point ominously towards the disaster which is to befall, in a line such as 'May the winds blow till they have wakened death!' We feel that the winds of malice and envy are gathering force even as he speaks. Desdemona (whose name means 'evil fate') is often associated with death in the play and Othello's allusion to his own death falls on our ears with an ominously different sense from that which it has for the ecstatic speaker:

> *If it were now to die,*
> *'Twere now to be most happy; for I fear*
> *My soul hath her content so absolute*
> *That not another comfort like to this*
> *Succeeds in unknown fate.*

We fear too, but literally, not figuratively, and the last line of the encounter between the lovers does nothing to reassure us: 'Once more well met at Cyprus'.

The change to Iago's brisk and workmanlike prose recalls us again to a different world. Notice that Iago's regard for Roderigo is so low that he does not scruple to refer to him as a 'base' man even as he blandly tells him that 'Desdemona is directly in love with him [Cassio]' which he probably knows to be a lie though in his soliloquy at the end of the scene he pretends to believe it. But we must beware of loathing Iago simply because he seems to loathe everyone else. We may rather learn from him how easily and groundlessly one may proceed from misjudgement to condemnation. It may help if we notice that the line of argument Iago now puts to Roderigo, though it is couched in far less reputable terms, is not essentially different from one which Othello has already used in his defence. 'She loved me for the dangers I had passed' he has declared, 'and I loved her that she did pity them'. On Iago's lips this becomes 'she first loved the Moor, but for bragging and telling her fantastical lies'. And what Brabantio had attributed to witchcraft, Iago asserts to be mere sensuality and a taste for the exotic, neither of which can last very long. Cassio's availability and presentability make him, according to Iago, the obvious choice when the time comes. If we are prompted to reject this reading of the situation, it is because of the fulness and candour with which, in our sight and that of all Venice and Cyprus, the lovers have committed themselves to each other. But before we condemn Iago out of hand we should recognize that if we had not ourselves seen and heard Othello and Desdemona his words would have a deadly plausibility, and it is because we have seen and heard Cassio that we realize that Iago's description of him is really a description of the speaker himself:

> *A slipper and subtle knave, a finder out of occasions; that has an eye can stamp and counterfeit advantages, though true advantage never present itself; a devilish knave!*

The more Iago insists that only a black man's lechery and an over-refined and bored white girl's taste for kinky sexual thrills are in question, the more we are aware of an inner necessity in this man which drives him to believe that people are like this and only like this and can never be otherwise. In a fine essay W. H. Auden called Iago a kind of Baconian scientist, ready to put Othello's nature on the rack of experimental investigation. But behind the apparent objectivity is a raging desire, not to find out whether what he believes is true, but to twist the evidence to suit his pre-formed convictions. In this Iago is only the most extreme example of a tendency we have already seen in Brabantio and are to see most tragically in Othello himself, a tendency from which even the most scientifically minded among us are not entirely free.

What is courtesy to Roderigo (and to us) is lechery to Iago even though, unlike ourselves, Roderigo is predisposed to believe him. In any case he has neither the intelligence nor the spirit to withstand Iago's rhetoric. From Iago's soliloquy at the end of the scene we learn more about him than he wishes to tell us. The need to justify himself is apparent in the very first lines, as is his frank avowal of Othello's true nature. His declaration 'Now I do love her too' rings hollowly in our ears, perhaps in his own, and is immediately displaced by his need for revenge for being allegedly cuckolded by Othello. What was a rumour casually mentioned in the earlier soliloquy has hardened, or so he claims, into a definite suspicion. There *is* something 'the thought whereof/Doth, like a poisonous mineral, gnaw my inwards'. The passionate language indicates that. Iago needs to justify his plot against Cassio with an aside which sounds even less convincing than the charge against Othello: 'For I fear Cassio with my nightcap too'. But, as with the first soliloquy, the last lines reveal the genuine impulse behind all the self-justification: a desire to be admired for his cunning and for his improvisatory skills.

One of the effects of Iago's presence in the play, therefore, is that he makes it impossible to look at and listen to any of it with innocent eyes and ears. Even when we are not fully aware of the details of his scheming, a sense of dramatic irony pervades all the action almost to the very end, because by being taken into the villain's confidence, we have been made in some degree his accomplices.

Act II, Scene 2

Even the brief scene of the Herald's proclamation inviting the citizenry to celebrate the recent victory and the general's nuptials link the public and the domestic action of the play, as they were linked in the Senate scene. The invitation to 'each man to what sports and revels his addiction leads him' may remind us of the 'sports and revels' which one man's 'addiction' has just led him to reveal to us.

Act II, Scene 3

Othello's gentle warning to Cassio 'not to outsport discretion' has a more menacing sound because of Iago's words and it is the reverse of reassuring to learn that Iago himself has been left in charge because 'Iago is most honest'.

The Herald's proclamation, amongst other things, marks a change of tempo between the scenes it divides. The rhythm and tone of this last scene, after the grave courtesy of Othello's speech with Cassio and Desdemona, moves into a kind of uneasy bantering. Cassio repeatedly fobs off Iago's attempts to make coarse conversation, as between two soldiers, about their commander's wedding night. Phrases like 'made wanton the night', 'sport for Jove' and 'full of game' are resolutely stone-walled with others like 'she is a most exquisite lady', 'she's a most fresh and delicate creature' and finally 'she is indeed perfection'. Having been thwarted in his bid to establish a soldierly camaraderie with his intended victim Iago turns boldly to the main task in hand, linking his invitation to have a drink with the presence of two local citizens anxious to drink 'to the health of black Othello'. Cassio's protests are predictably short-lived and the scene quickly develops into a drinking match with just enough time for Iago to tell us that he has already primed several local gallants to take on Cassio should he challenge them in his drink. We notice again Iago's capacity to profit from accidental details which he cannot exactly foresee but is determined to turn to his advantage. Very soon he will use this skill to momentous and tragic effect.

The drinking scene is a good example of the way in which Iago's presence and our 'complicity' with him prevents us from taking at face value what should be a moment of jollity and relaxation. The song and the chaff about the drinking propensities of various nations are good-humoured enough, but our attention is focused on the effect they have on

27

Cassio whose drunken utterances forebode what is to come: 'I hold him to be unworthy of his place that does those things'.

As Iago himself has been at pains to tell us, the gulling of Roderigo is hardly a worthy object for his sinister talents. With Cassio he has a more intelligent though unwitting opponent. But the ease with which in this scene Cassio succumbs first to Iago's persuasion and then to a drunken rage reveals Iago's technique of ascertaining a person's weakness and then exploiting it in the guise of a concerned and loyal companion; it also paves the way for his final and deadliest triumph. Thus the successive deceptions of Roderigo, Cassio and Othello mark the ascending progress of Iago's villainy. But we must remember that they are only the climactic moments of a general tendency to hoodwink the whole of Venice (including his own wife) which have earned him the universal and wholly undeserved soubriquet of 'honest Iago'.

Montano's response when told by Iago of Cassio's alleged weak head for drink is heavy with irony:

> ... 'tis great pity that the noble Moor
> Should hazard such a place as his own second
> With one of an ingraft infirmity.
> It were an honest action to say
> So to the Moor.

'It were' indeed 'an honest action' to tell Othello in whom precisely his trust is utterly misplaced, but only the audience knows the truth and they (we) are of course unable to help, which accounts for the mounting frustration we begin to feel from now on. After this conversation the action moves swiftly in a series of rapid, broken and confused exchanges which reach a dramatic period in the ringing of the bell, the traditional warning of fire or other peril to the community, and the re-entry of Othello immediately afterwards. Iago at once slides into the role of solicitous assistant to his commander – 'Have you forgot all sense of place and duty?' – and restorer of order. Othello's speech makes clear how much more than an ordinary drunken brawl this is, taking place as it does on an island only just freed from the threat of war. He turns naturally for an explanation to 'honest Iago' who, right on cue, 'looks dead with grieving' and at first shows the utmost reluctance to say anything, except that he cannot understand how it all happened, though he makes it clear that he saw everything. It is a stroke of luck for Iago that Montano is too badly hurt to give his own account of what happened, but it is the kind of luck that Iago has helped to make for himself. In the lines beginning 'Now, by heaven,/My blood begins my safer guides to rule' Othello reveals an aspect of himself that we shall recall later. Once again he stresses the irresponsibility of starting a brawl when the town is in such a tense condition. Othello's resolution, impartiality and keen sense of responsibility as commander of a troubled island are evident here. Iago is again called upon, as the only impartial witness available, to give his own account of the matter, and Montano's warning to him not to be swayed by partiality for Cassio plays into his hands. As we would expect, Iago appears to be deeply affected by this. But his account, while appearing to be extorted from him with the utmost unwillingness, makes Cassio's dereliction of duty damningly clear. He will display the same reluctance to even more devastating effect when he 'allows' Othello to 'extort' from him the 'truth' about Desdemona. Iago does not scruple to mingle downright lies with half-truths in his story, as when he says that Roderigo first came in crying for help, and our grudging admiration is given to the way in which, while getting Cassio into the deepest trouble with his commanding officer, he yet manages to appear Cassio's devoted friend. By this time, perhaps, we are beginning to be a little impatient of Othello's repeated references to Iago's honesty, but it is as well to remember that Othello is not alone in this and to ask ourselves how *we* would have reacted to his narration. This is a test which Iago constantly imposes on us.

It may be Desdemona's brief appearance at this point which puts into Iago's head the notion of prompting Cassio to ask Desdemona to plead with Othello for the restitution of his lost command. He had said nothing of this in his last soliloquy though he had certainly some scheme in his mind to entrap Cassio and Desdemona ever since he saw them conversing familiarly by the harbour. He feels his way carefully into Cassio's confidence when they are left alone, and we can hardly help noticing the irony of the one man in Venice whose very survival depends on 'reputation' decrying it in such round terms. As often, Iago speaks the exact truth, confident that his hero will not believe him: 'Reputation is an idle and most false imposition; oft got without merit and lost without deserving'.

Throughout the play we observe a close but ironic relationship between real and metaphorical wounds which comes to its climax in the very last moments of the tragedy. Having carefully ascertained that Cassio cannot identify his assailant, Iago now puts into the latter's head the notion that Desdemona has such power over her husband that if he can make her take up his case, success is certain. Here too, the praise he gives Desdemona, 'so blessed a disposition she holds it a vice in her goodness not to do more than she is requested', is quite true, though ominous for us in its implications. Cassio swallows the bait whole; is there any good reason why he should not? His confession, 'I am desperate of my fortunes if they check me here', gives us a fleeting insight into the precarious livelihood of the professional mercenary in the seventeenth century. Once more we are left alone with our confidant 'honest Iago' whose opening line is a challenge flung directly and defiantly at us: 'And what's he then that says I play the villain?' Carefully avoiding any question of evil intent, which most of us would regard as fairly important in judging villainy, he concentrates on justifying himself by the 'objective' soundness of the advice he has just given. According to him, it is the simple truth that to go through Desdemona is the quickest way to make Othello change his mind, because her influence over her husband is all but absolute. How then can he be accused of villainy in his advice to Cassio? Iago may want to fool us but he is beyond fooling himself, for he answers his rhetorical question immediately. He knows exactly what his villainy consists of and does not hesitate to tell us, for, like most great artists, he has an insatiable thirst for applause. Observe how Iago has appropriated the term everyone uses about him to his own purposes. Three times in this soliloquy he uses the word 'honest', first to mean 'straightforward' (clearly ironic), then in an unironic way to mean 'above board' (with a suggestion of sexual probity as well) and finally in a totally contemptuous and characteristic fashion, signifying little more than 'credulous' or merely 'foolish'. The imagery of poison to signify the action of malicious rumour and unfounded jealousy occurs throughout the play, while Iago's closing lines have an application wider than his reference to Desdemona, for in this tragedy as in some others by Shakespeare, it is the victims' virtue rather than their weakness which brings about their destruction.

There is an instantly felt contrast between the confident and vigorous accents of Iago and Roderigo's ineffectual moaning. Iago's sententious reply to him is yet another example of his habit of generalizing and also reveals his real relish for his own devious expertise. The act closes with Iago giving us another statement of intent, increasing suspense and tightening our anxiety another notch. At this point in the play we are no longer in any doubt about Iago's nature and intentions. The deception of Roderigo, which continues almost to the end of the play, and of Cassio have given us a taste of Iago's methods and we are keenly apprehensive about the ability of his final victim to withstand his wiles.

Act III, Scene 1

The opening of the third act, with its music, provides a brief interlude, not so much to relieve our anxieties as to transpose them to another key. The comic dialogue between the musicians and the clown was doubtless intended for the same purpose, but not even the bawdy jokes about tails and wind instruments prevent this exchange from falling on our ears with a dull and deadening thud. Though skilled actors may make something of it, it is usually omitted in performance and not often missed. Of all Shakespeare's clowns, surely this one deserves the prize for the most dismal.

The real business of the scene begins with Iago's entrance. His opening remark, 'You have not been abed then!', gives us an impression of the continuous flow of time and hence of unimpeded action. Much has been written about the two mutually inconsistent time schemes in *Othello*, one wherein all the action takes place in a single sweep of less than two days from the elopement and the voyage to Cyprus until the final disaster, the other involving a much longer period in which Desdemona, for instance, allegedly had time to be unfaithful with Cassio more than once. Only two things need to be said on this matter here. The first is that there undoubtedly are discrepancies in the time scheme of the play. The second is that these matter not at all either in reading or in performance, for we do not notice them. Shakespeare was a master of the theatrical use of time and for this particular tragedy he needed a combination of two kinds of time, the leisurely and the hectic, so he used both with no regard for consistency. What we respond to is the accelerating pace of the action as it rushes towards its destined end.

This scene introduces us to Iago's wife Emilia, an important figure in the action. Although her speech here is mainly concerned with providing essential information and keeping the plot moving, some of the candour and kindliness of the speaker comes out in her plain, unpretentious words. We also gather, from the fact that she is allowed to remain while husband and wife are discussing Cassio, that she is more Desdemona's confidante than her maidservant. We may be heartened, listening to her, by a hope that all may yet be well and that Cassio will regain his former position. Such feelings are part of our normal theatrical experience however familiar we may be with the play. But given the general atmosphere of cunning evil pitted against unsuspecting innocence, our hope must be faint indeed. While Emilia is perfectly sincere in her desire to help Cassio, as shown in her final lines, we know that she is acting unwittingly as Iago's instrument.

Act III, Scene 2

This very short exchange between Othello and Iago shows Othello assuming his public duties with Iago still firmly entrenched as a trusty deputy. Short schemes such as this one and the Herald's proclamation contribute to the impression of swiftly moving action. All the principal characters in Iago's plot have now been introduced to us and the long scene which follows shows them becoming slowly but inextricably entangled in the web of Iago's venomous hate.

Act III, Scene 3

With this very long scene, almost every word and pause of which repays our closest attention, we come to the very heart of the play. Knowing what we do, we cannot fail to be uneasy at Desdemona's confident assertion that it will only be a matter of time before Cassio regains his command, while the irony of Emilia's remark about how concerned her husband is over the matter is all the more powerful because it is literally true. Cassio's words show not only his loyal devotion to Desdemona but a dignified and manly statement of his case, namely that unless his office is restored soon, it may be too late. Desdemona's response ought to give us pause to consider how far she is justified in her attitude. It ends with her resolve, half jokingly expressed no doubt, but full of irony for all that, to die rather than let Cassio down. It is of course wholly admirable that she intends to keep whatever promise she makes, but has she the right to declare boldly to Cassio 'I give thee warrant of thy place'? Desdemona speaks with the confidence born of absolute and unquestioning love. But Cassio has been dismissed by his duly authorized commanding officer for what the latter has judged to be a grave breach of discipline at a time of emergency. The commanding officer's wife now calmly proposes to plague him night and day until he reverses his decision, without, as far as we know, having bothered even to find out how far Cassio was to blame. Whatever this may tell us about Desdemona's power over Othello, it shows little understanding of or regard for the responsibilities of her husband's position. We shall be put in mind more than once as the action develops of this running together of public and private duties and attachments. It is therefore important to understand just what is involved in Othello's response to his wife's plea later in the scene.

Before we reach that point, however, there is a brief but crucial moment whose significance would have been plain on the Jacobean stage, with its deep acting area and two entrance/exit doors at the back. As Othello and Iago enter at one of these, Emilia, who has probably been standing diagonally downstage with Desdemona and Cassio, draws attention to the arrival of the other two. Cassio then makes a hasty exit by the other door, passing Othello and Iago as they are walking downstage; the entire width of the stage is between Cassio and the other two men as they pass. This gives plausibility to Iago's masterly pretended aside: 'Ha! I like not that' as well as to Othello's uncertainty as to whether it really was Cassio who had just left, and to Iago's poisonously false insistence that it could not have been Cassio who would 'steal away so guilty-like'. No doubt there would be something awkward and embarrassed about Cassio's exit, but it takes an Iago to sow in Othello's mind the idea that there was anything sinister or underhand about it. With those very first phrases, 'Ha! I like not that' and 'Nothing, my lord; or if – I know not what', with their feigned perplexity and reluctance, Iago has already begun, as he has promised, to pour his pestilence into Othello's ear.

From this point onwards, things go exactly as Iago would wish. Desdemona immediately launches into her appeal on behalf of Cassio, with Iago's talk of Cassio's 'guilty-like' departure still sounding unquietly somewhere in the back of Othello's mind. In this situation, Desdemona's words cannot be altogether welcome and we are not surprised to find that her husband's first concern is to establish that it really was Cassio who had just left. Desdemona now unwisely adopts a wheedling, importunate manner, asking Othello to name a definite date for Cassio's reinstatement, exactly calculated to wear Othello's resistance down while at the same time, unbeknown to Desdemona, it stirs her husband's still barely felt misgivings. We may note once more that Desdemona's case rests on a total confusion of personal feelings with official duties; Cassio should be pardoned for a military offence because he has been their good friend. For good measure she even makes the reinstatement of Cassio a move in a projected game of marital tit-for-tat, boldly asking

> *I wonder in my soul*
> *What you would ask me that I should deny,*
> *Or stand so mammering on?*

No wonder Othello caves in without even reminding her that she should not interfere in official matters, especially in total ignorance of the relevant facts. (Her indifference to just what may have happened is striking.) If we have any sympathy for those Romans in *Antony and*

Cleopatra who condemn Antony for letting his generalship be weakened by his infatuation (and Antony condemns himself for this), we should realize that Desdemona is doing exactly the same thing. But in mitigation we may say that Desdemona, on the strength of her knowledge of Cassio, judges him to be fundamentally incapable of doing a serious wrong even though he may be technically guilty. This is an example of implicit judgement based on one kind of 'evidence', that of intimate personal acquaintance; it is radically opposed to Iago's generalizing, pseudo-scientific sort of evaluation.

From the moment of Othello's entrance in this scene our attention is fixed on how he responds to the various pressures on him, first that of Desdemona and then those of Iago. There is a moment of relief for us when Othello appears to have yielded, but it can be a moment only, for Iago has only just begun to go to work. Desdemona's mildly coquettish speech to the effect that she is merely asking what her husband himself really wants is strangely discordant with Othello's own repeated 'I will deny thee nothing' which seems an uneasy mixture of resigned assent, a touch of condescension, and more than a touch of weariness and impatience. But his plea to her to 'leave me a little to myself' already shows that feeling of bewilderment at her interference in professional matters which is one of the many uncertainties which Iago will ruthlessly exploit.

Desdemona's coquettishness is with her to the end, but her lines 'Be as your fancies teach you./Whate'er you be, I am obedient' are frighteningly prophetic of the ensuing tragedy. We do not of course know this, but we can surely catch a hint of it in Desdemona's playfulness, Othello's acquiescence (it is, after all, *he* who has promised to 'obey' *her*) and Iago's watchful silence.

After our first experience of the play we realize that *Othello* is a tragedy more than usually charged with proleptic irony, that is, irony which works by looking forward to future developments. Perhaps the most notable instance of this kind of irony occurs in the lines Othello now speaks, which may not be entirely free from a sense of foreboding even for the speaker himself, although he may utter them for reassurance:

> *Excellent wretch! Perdition catch my soul*
> *But I do love thee! And when I love thee not,*
> *Chaos is come again.*

The swiftly moving events of the rest of the play will show us that Othello here speaks nothing but the dreadful literal truth.

The stage is now clear for Iago to administer further doses of his deadly poison and watch as it takes effect, with ourselves as his fascinated 'accomplices'. He begins with an innocent-sounding inquiry as to whether Cassio knew of the Othello–Desdemona romance, formally distancing the object of his inquiry from himself by using both Cassio's names, as if he was asking a question in court. His refusal at first to give a direct answer to Othello's question 'Why dost thou ask?' is characteristic of a main part of his technique, which is to pretend to know much more than he says, but to be reluctant to speak the awful truth for fear of causing pain to the hearer. Another feature of his method, almost as important as the first, is the use of apparently meaningful repetition, seen here in his repetition of 'indeed' and of Othello's 'honest' and 'think'. Tension rises in the brief 'liney' exchange between the two; as Othello becomes more impatient and Iago increasingly cagey, Othello's impatience explodes in an outburst which makes it clear that Iago's technique has succeeded completely:

> *By heaven, he echoes me,*
> *As if there were some monster in his thought*
> *Too hideous to be shown.*

Anyone who has seen a good horror movie knows that a monster recognized only by the havoc it wreaks (and perhaps by the odd enormous footprint) is much more exciting than a monster with all the polystyrene and luminous paint showing. Iago, like a skilful film director, not only suggests the monster to his intended victim, but prompts him actually to create the monster from within the imagination, where the most fearful monsters are born. We realize that Iago's questions and his reactions to Othello's answers have remained imprinted in Othello's mind from Othello's account of Iago's demeanour (the lines are also, of course, a set of stage directions for the actor playing Iago) and how poignantly close he comes to the truth when he speaks of Iago having 'some horrible conceit' shut up within him. With his injunction to Iago to 'show me thy thought' (which may remind us of what Iago said about never letting his 'outward action' reveal 'the native act and figure' of his heart), Othello is already lost. But Iago bides his time and 'plays' his victim with caution and cunning, eliciting from Othello yet another tribute to his love and honesty. Here Othello shows his capacity, as he supposes, to recognize hypocritical displays of loyalty in a villain, but the irony is that he puts Iago in the wrong one of his two categories of 'false, disloyal knave' and 'the just man', taking as spontaneous sincerity what is only the artful simulation of it – a mistake that, as we have seen, most people make about

35

Iago. It becomes increasingly clear that at a very deep and comprehensive level *Othello* is a play about the hazards of judging people, and the way our bases of judgement are likely to be distorted when the people concerned are especially close to us. That Othello becomes a victim of jealousy is undeniable; that this shows him to be more than ordinarily foolish, gullible or self-concerned does not follow by any means. Jealousy may be a sign of the strength of love or its weakness, but in either case Othello is less foolish than many critics who see in his attitude only folly and egoism.

It is because Othello has already imagined in his inmost self the possibility of Desdemona's loss that Iago can exploit his secret fear so easily. The apparent effortlessness should not, however, blind us to the precision and expertness with which he does it. The seemingly straightforward tribute to Cassio's honesty – 'I dare be sworn I think that he is honest' – is anything but straightforward. The passive construction and the roundabout phrasing hint at doubt without expressing it, but the hinting is enough to provoke Othello's perplexed affirmation: 'I think so too'. Iago then launches into a generalized wish which, without any direct mention of Cassio, insinuates that he may be one of those who 'be not what they seem'. When, after Othello's somewhat bewildered, or perhaps somewhat impatient assent to this proposition, Iago repeats his conviction that he 'thinks' Cassio is an honest man, the assertion sounds as if it meant something less or other than it appears to, and Othello does not fail to see that 'yet there's more in this'. The terms in which he now urges Iago to speak his mind are significant: 'give thy worst of thoughts/ The worst of words.'

He is evidently much more than half prepared to hear evil tidings of Cassio and Iago's earlier linking of Cassio and Desdemona is perhaps not far below the surface of his thoughts. We remember how unused he has been to any romantic relationship and the feelings involved in it. Iago responds with the familiar yet highly effective trick of being reluctant to speak his mind. His claim that he is entitled to keep his thoughts to himself, coming at this point, predictably increases Othello's desire to know what he is thinking, particularly as Iago implies that his thoughts are too horrible for utterance. The metaphor of the palace into which vile things may sometimes intrude is a strikingly ironic reminder to us of what is happening here. The noble palace of Othello's mind is being infected with the rank sewage of Iago's innuendo; yet we see that Othello, any more than the rest of us, does not have 'a breast so pure' that it is totally immune to 'some uncleanly apprehensions'.

Othello now anxiously cooperates in creating the monster that will destroy him by expressing the possibility that he may be 'wronged'. He is now convinced that whatever Iago knows touches him, Othello, personally, and that only loyalty and the desire not to wound his commanding officer prevent him from speaking. And all this when Iago has said practically nothing except that he believes Cassio to be an honest man!

Having put Othello in a position where disclosing what Iago 'knows' becomes a matter of the latter's love and loyalty, Iago enjoys himself by telling Othello the exact truth – 'my jealousy shapes faults that are not' – and by begging the Moor to do what he now knows to be impossible for him: take no notice of what Iago says. We are fascinated and appalled by the audacity of the torturer who can plainly say to his victim:

> *It were not for your quiet nor your good, ..*
> *To let you know my thoughts.*

When Othello asks why, Iago launches into another generalized oration, this time on the theme of reputation or 'good name' which we, having heard him hold forth on the same subject to Cassio, know to be a façade of falsehood. The fact that what he says is mostly true does not, of course, detract from his evil purpose in saying it at this time to this man. Othello is now near distraction, convinced that his 'good name' is threatened or besmirched in some way unknown to him: 'By heaven, I'll know thy thoughts!' As we have seen earlier, Othello's reputation, both public and personal, means a great deal to him. He relies, as on a suit of invincible armour, on 'my parts, my title, and my perfect soul'. He literally cannot survive when this perfection is endangered. But Iago knows his man and counters with a flat refusal to speak his 'thoughts'. Othello's 'Ha!' is a cry of impatient fury which evokes another typically sententious speech, on jealousy and its perils. Coming immediately after the speech on reputation, the implications are as clear as they are ominous for Othello's peace of mind. Now for the first time Iago feels confident enough to speak of cuckolds, and of the comparative comfort of ignorant cuckoldry. He also foreshadows Othello's impending fate as one 'Who dotes, yet doubts – suspects, yet strongly loves!' Iago's explicit and eloquent speeches such as this one are all the more effective for the reluctantly uttered phrases and the silences with which they are interspersed. They seem to come from the depths of worldly experience as well as of loyalty. Having reduced Othello to fearful grief – 'O misery!' – he pursues his advantage with a pious prayer that he may always be free from the torment of jealousy.

Perhaps there is a brief pause at this point while Othello makes a valiant effort to shake himself free from the slimy snare of Iago's insinuations. Othello reveals his own decisive nature (so unlike that of Hamlet, for instance) in his statement, 'to be once in doubt/Is once to be resolved', and there is a hideous anticipatory irony in the words that immediately follow:

> *Exchange me for a goat,*
> *When I shall turn the business of my soul*
> *To such exsufflicate and blown surmises,*
> *Matching thy inference.*

The sense of his words indicates a determination *not* to be taken in by Iago's foul aspersions, but the imagery of goats and blow-flies battening on carrion already shows the extent to which his language (and therefore his imagination) has been corrupted by the beastliness of the Iago outlook. However, in the touching and tender tribute which Othello pays to his wife immediately afterwards, we see more ground than we have yet found in this scene for hope that the noble Moor can yet recover himself. Certainly there is a proud confidence in the simple declaration 'For she had eyes, and chose me' which looks back to the time when his feelings for Desdemona were based on his own immediate experience of her rather than the worldly-wise generalities which he has been fed. If only Othello could keep faith with that commitment and conviction all might yet be well. But we dare not formulate that hope, particularly since the speech ends with the assumption that 'proof' of guilt may be found in the case. Once more we note that it is Othello not Iago who has specifically mentioned his wife in the context of possible infidelity. Those critics who claim that Othello is digging his own pit through fear and jealousy and that Iago is not much more than a device for pushing him into it are guilty of minimizing both Iago's skill and his creative villainy. But their under-estimation of Iago points to an important truth: without a predisposition on Othello's part to believe the worst, there would have been no tragedy.

Iago now enters completely into the role of devoted and outspoken friend. His words 'I speak not yet of proof' imply that at some later stage proof would be forthcoming. What does and does not constitute proof in a given case is one of the central questions of the play and determines much of its action. What is the proof that the Turkish fleet has sailed away? What is the proof that Desdemona has been bewitched? Or that Cassio has defaulted in his duty? Or that Iago is devoted to Roderigo's cause? These and many other questions involving the topic of proof prepare us for the final, central and tragic question: what is the proof of

Desdemona's guilt? Othello fatally forgets that there can be other kinds of proof than the legal and the scientific; for *him*, the fact that Desdemona had eyes and chose him should have been confirmation of her love and fidelity as strong as proofs of holy writ. When he allows himself to be ensnared into looking for pseudo-legal proof of her guilt, he has already gone far towards convicting her in the tribunal of his mind.

Iago's bold advice to Othello: 'Look to your wife; observe her well with Cassio' is an indication of how strong his hold over the Moor now is; he can actually set the husband to spy on the wife. What is more, he even goes so far as to instruct Othello in his outward demeanour: 'Wear your eye thus'. But what he asks is a physical impossibility. If you love someone you cannot treat her as the object of a clinical experiment and be totally detached, however hard you try: 'not jealous or secure'. Merely to look for signs of disloyalty in one you love is to come perilously close to finding them, or thinking you have found them, because no mind, least of all Othello's, can rest in uncertainties on such a matter. And the pity of it is that, as Othello himself has said earlier in the scene, the way you interpret evidence about a person often depends on your *prior* evaluation of the person concerned. Iago claims to base his advice on a thorough knowledge of the place he is talking about, and it is perhaps helpful to remember that in the seventeenth century Venice had a reputation, among other things, for sexual licence, Venetian courtesans being noted for their elegance and professional sophistication:

> *I know our country disposition well:*
> *In Venice they do let God see the pranks*
> *They dare not show their husbands; their best conscience*
> *Is not to leave't undone, but keep't unknown.*

This is calculated to undermine Othello's psychological security further, as he is a stranger to this sophisticated society, his background being the very different one of strange places and people – 'antres vast and deserts idle' and 'men whose heads/Do grow beneath their shoulders' – and his experience of life being based more in the battlefield than the bedroom: 'moving accidents by flood and field'. With Othello thus inwardly shaken, Iago now makes the brilliantly daring move of using the very fact which had earlier been Othello's firm anchorage – 'she had eyes and chose me' – as an argument for Desdemona's deceptiveness: 'she did deceive her father, marrying you'. When Othello assents to this he has unwittingly helped to drive yet another nail into the coffin where his love and peace of mind are soon to lie buried.

Perhaps Iago feels that he is pressing his advantage too fast and too directly with his reference to 'she that, so young, could give out such a seeming' for he changes tack abruptly, appearing to blame himself 'for too much loving you'. Othello's troubled reply, 'I am bound to thee for ever', is of course profoundly ironic. His mind is further perplexed by the need to deny to Iago that he *is* troubled. Cunningly Iago now puts into Othello's mind what he hopes will be the effect of his suggestions by pretending to desire the exact opposite:

> *I am to pray you, not to strain my speech*
> *To grosser issues, nor to larger reach*
> *Than to suspicion.*

Given what he himself had earlier said about the mental agony of one who 'dotes, yet doubts – suspects, yet strongly loves' and his express advice to Othello not to 'build yourself a trouble out of my scattering and unsure observance' we can well imagine what the effect of these words will be on the Moor. In fact Iago uses Othello's answer, 'I will not', to speculate on what would happen if Othello were to fail in his resolve, and so keeps that possibility feverishly active in Othello's imagination. He then again introduces, seemingly quite innocently, a reference to Cassio, 'my worthy friend', and compels Othello to respond with a conviction, somewhat half-hearted to be sure, of Desdemona's honesty (faithfulness). How much less than certain Othello now is appears, however, after Iago's pious yet double-edged exclamation: 'Long live she so! and long live you to think so!' The grammatically incomplete line which Othello now utters marks with the finest precision almost the very moment when Iago's poison penetrates so deep into Othello's consciousness that recovery is all but impossible: 'And yet, how nature erring from itself –'.

The first thing we notice is that the thought half-expressed here belongs to a vastly different realm of feeling from that on which Othello's inner peace depends and without which chaos is indeed come again – that, given Desdemona's unique nature, her free choice of him was for her the most 'natural' thing in the world. Secondly, Othello is here in virtual agreement with Brabantio's view that Desdemona's behaviour in choosing her husband was unnatural and must have been effected by sinister means. Indeed, Brabantio uses the same key words: 'nature' and 'err':

> *It is a judgement maimed and most imperfect*
> *That will confess perfection so could err*
> *Against all rules of nature . . .*

Iago is naturally quick to seize the point and elaborate it with savage relish: 'Foh! One may smell in such a will most rank/Foul disproportion, thoughts unnatural –'. But again he realizes he may have gone too far and asks Othello's pardon. However, he is confident enough to make the insulting suggestion that Desdemona's 'better judgement' may lead her to repent her marriage when she has had time to compare her husband with her own countrymen. It is a measure of how far his suggestions have been tacitly accepted by his victim that Othello makes no reply to the comment that Iago is only speaking of Desdemona as a *typical* Venetian woman (Iago's usual approach to people and things) whereas it was on the perception of mutual uniqueness that their love was founded. He actually encourages Iago not only to spy on Desdemona himself but to set his wife to spy on her as well. Left alone for a moment, Othello makes it plain that the evil work has been thoroughly accomplished, for he already regrets his marriage and is convinced that Iago knows more than he is willing to disclose. Iago re-enters briefly to turn the knife in the wound once more by imploring Othello to 'scan this thing no further', only to conclude by asking Othello himself to spy on his wife. For good measure, to use an inapt phrase, he makes sure that Cassio's reinstatement is delayed, thus converting Desdemona's pleas on his behalf into damning evidence of her guilt as far as Othello is concerned. Othello's words 'Fear not my government' make us do exactly that, for we fear that his 'government' (self-discipline) will collapse under the strain of the evil force bearing down on it.

By now we may be more than a little tired of hearing about Iago's 'exceeding honesty'. The metaphor of the trained falcon and the falconer which Othello now uses to represent the relationship between himself and his wife is not likely to fall sympathetically on modern ears. But we must remember that for Shakespeare's original audience male dominance was a necessary and accepted condition of the marital relationship. This does not necessarily mean that Shakespeare accepted it passively as such. As with other accepted notions (the association of black men with lust and cruelty, for instance) Shakespeare often used the assumptions of his audience in order to subvert them. Othello's musings reveal some of the sources of his insecurity: that he is black, that he has not the sophisticated social manners of the Venetian gallants (such as Roderigo, presumably!), and that he is old (we remember that he was Desdemona's father's friend and guest). His inner sense of himself has been subjected to such vicious and violent onslaughts that he is willing to submit himself mentally to the crudest of sorting processes: colour, class and age. But these factors were equally applicable at the time Desdemona chose him and were doubtless given due consideration then.

It may be objected that we should not be speculating about what characters in a play may or may not have done in scenes which are not actually portrayed, since this would take us away from the play before us to a realm of unverifiable speculation. Dramatic characters, we are asked to remember, have their life in the play and nowhere else. This last point is self-evidently true but it does not follow that all speculation on characters' motives and actions other than those actually depicted on stage is irrelevant or impermissible. To understand fully what a character says or does at a given moment, it may often be necessary to assume some earlier course of action or reflection on his or her part. Here, it seems clear that the points Othello touched on have been discussed before, because we cannot imagine the marriage taking place without such discussion, without doing violence to our sense of the two lovers and their relationship. There are several occasions in the play when such speculation, kept within reasonable bounds, will enlarge our understanding of what is going on; we should not be frightened off it by abstract theorizing.

Much more ominous is Othello's bald declaration: 'She's gone' followed by the equally bare assertion 'I am abused'. We now understand Othello's earlier words, 'To be once in doubt is once to be resolved', in a different and more frightening sense. Othello literally cannot bear being unsure on a matter such as this and his fevered imagination dislocates fact and fancy, past and future, projecting not only his worst fears as accomplished reality but accompanying the projection with the appropriate emotional response: 'I am abused, and my relief/Must be to loathe her.' Already he has adopted not only Iago's animal imagery to describe human conduct but also Iago's habit of making sweeping statements about human conduct, discarding that subjective personal knowledge of an individual human being on which alone love and trust are based. 'O, curse of marriage' he cries, 'That we can call these delicate creatures ours,/And not their appetites!'

But of course Othello is not 'we' and he has no plural number of 'delicate creatures' to call his. He is a single unique individual, and his blackness and exotic background are as much a symbol of this uniqueness as anything else, and there is one single unique human being whom he has chosen and who has publicly and privately chosen him. When each declares and acts out of that commitment – Desdemona before the Signiory, both at their first meeting in Cyprus, Othello in his words to her after the night time brawl – we feel them to be speaking and acting out of their inmost selves. But when that absolute commitment, prompted not by statistical probability but based on a clear-eyed individual choice, is undermined, chaos and destruction are not far off. That is why even the mere hunt for 'evidence' is fatal to the existence and integrity of a relationship based on evidence of a totally different kind. Othello's words, ''Tis destiny unshunnable like death', have a particular meaning tragically narrower in scope than the wide generalization he attempts to make of them. And the Iago-like habit of sweeping statement rapidly becomes a means of evading individual responsibility while, ironically, increasing individual suffering.

Now follows the central incident of the play, pathetically trivial and momentously tragic at once. Once more the actual existential presence of Desdemona is sufficient to dispel all Othello's ugly suspicions:

> *If she be false, O, then heaven mocks itself!*
> *I'll not believe't.*

The 'pain upon my forehead' may be an allusion, the reverse of comic in the circumstances although it occurs frequently in comedies, to the idea that horns sprouted in a cuckold's head. But it is perhaps more plausibly seen as an expression of Othello's real mental anguish. Emilia's words as she picks up the fallen handkerchief tell us several important things: that it was Othello's first gift to Desdemona; that he has charged Desdemona to take special care of it, which she has done; and that Iago has often asked Emilia to steal it. The fact that Emilia has been unwilling to steal the handkerchief but is not averse to 'borrowing' it without her mistress's knowledge and having the pattern copied for her husband tells us both about her practical worldly outlook and her genuine affection for her husband. But in this context her confession that 'What he will do with it heaven knows, not I' can only increase our anxiety.

In the late seventeenth century a lawyer named Thomas Rymer who thought *Othello* nothing more than 'a bloody farce' had some fun with this scene, declaring its moral to be 'a warning to all good wives, that they look well to their linen'. Perhaps the best way to defuse this kind of attack is to admit it and then point out how feeble its force is and how limited its applicability. If Desdemona had taken her customary care of the handkerchief, she would of course have retrieved it. Doubtless her concern for Othello's discomfort distracted her. That is all that needs to be said in answer to Rymer, though there is a good deal more to be said about the place of the handkerchief in the tragedy. But anyone who believes that the handkerchief was the central cause of the tragedy reveals the smallness of his imagination rather than that of the drama.

Desdemona's innocence is shown by, among other things, her immediate and simple assumption that Othello's 'pain' is entirely physical; hence her offer to bind his forehead with her handkerchief. But the 'napkin' that is rejected as 'too little' is to become the chief external instrument adding to Othello's torment. Again this underlines the vast gulf between the objective triviality and the psychologically determined subjective evaluation of what we take to be evidence.

The brief scene between Iago and Emilia conveys very economically the relationship between the two – the genuine feeling behind her flirtatiousness and the half-contemptuous affection on his part which is soon displaced by eagerness to possess the handkerchief in order to work further mischief: 'I have use for it'. Iago, as we have noted earlier, is a master of improvisation and the handkerchief offers ample scope for his talents. The famous lines he utters now embody much of what the play has to say about the way emotional need colours judgement and the appraisal of external 'facts':

> *Trifles light as air*
> *Are to the jealous confirmations strong*
> *As proofs of holy writ.*

We recognize the imagery of poison which follows as Iago's hallmark by now, together with the suggestion of the very depths of hell in 'the mines of sulphur'. The contrast in tone and resonance between these lines and the ones Iago speaks immediately on Othello's re-entry is striking. For a moment it seems as if Iago has unwittingly caught something of the power and scope of 'the Othello music':

> *Look where he comes! Not poppy, nor mandragora,*
> *Nor all the drowsy syrups of the world,*
> *Shall ever medicine thee to that sweet sleep*
> *Which thou owed'st yesterday.*

In poignant contrast, Othello is becoming more and more addicted to the venomous and bestial language of Iago with each passing moment. He swings crazily between the desire for blissful ignorance and the desperate consolation of knowing the imagined worst to be irrefutably true. This is the rack on which, as he truly says, Iago has set him. 'Othello's occupation's gone' because without emotional tranquillity he cannot exercise professional authority. We see now the full force of what Othello meant when he spoke of putting his 'free condition' into 'circumscription and confine' for love of Desdemona. The interwoven imagery of poison, torture and demonic possession (witchery) combines to bring powerfully before our imagination Othello's tragic predicament, and Othello's expression of it here unites the fast-fading rhetorical power of his 'music' with the new idiom of corruption and bestiality. What gives a distinctive strength to his language here is just this mixture, instanced by the juxtaposition of phrases indicative of his emotional attachment to his profession – the series that begins with 'Farewell the tranquil mind!' - with others of a very different sort: 'prove my love a whore!', 'better have been born a dog', and so on. A last faint glimmer of the truth, 'If thou dost slander her and torture me', only serves to highlight the blackness of the pit into which Othello has now fallen. 'I'll have some proof' he cries out, not doubting any longer that proof is to be found:

> *Her name that was as fresh*
> *As Dian's visage is now begrimed and black*
> *As mine own face.*

Othello has accepted Iago's evaluation of blackness as unnatural; even more dreadfully he demands: 'Villain, be sure thou prove my love a whore;/Be sure of it: give me ocular proof'.

Iago now plays with him as an angler plays a hooked fish, being elaborately sarcastic about the difficulty of actually showing Desdemona and her paramour *in flagrante delicto*. Othello no longer protests at the terms of the description except to demand 'a living reason she's disloyal' which elicits a downright but very effective lie from Iago about what Cassio had said and done in his sleep. The immediate result is that the roles are briefly and ironically reversed, with Iago trying to suggest that his 'evidence' may not be valid – 'Nay, this was but a dream' – and Othello convinced that it is conclusive: 'But this denoted a foregone conclusion'.

Iago then judges the time has come to play his trump card, the introduction of the handkerchief, complete with the detail, at once touching and sinister, about the pattern of strawberries which brings the 'trifle light as air' so vividly before us. He can now confidently talk of the final piece of 'evidence' as clinching the case, taken together 'with the other proofs'. So dazzled are we by his energetic confidence that we are almost betrayed, with Othello himself, into believing that there *have* been other proofs, rather than prurient insinuations and flat lies. Othello has now turned into an almost demented revenger, yet something of his former nobility still remains in lines like 'Yield up, O love, thy crown and hearted throne/To tyrannous hate' and the great speech that immediately follows.

The scene ends with a grotesque travesty of a chivalric pledge, with the 'knight' solemnly dedicating himself to the task before him and his 'squire' swearing allegiance to his master's cause. A further irony is of course that the roles of master and servant are reversed in reality; Iago is truly in command. Othello's language becomes irredeemably savage – 'Damn her, lewd minx! O damn her!' – and Iago's last line rings out with a literal truth more dreadful than anything Othello yet suspects: 'I am your own for ever'.

This is by far the longest scene in the play and in its structure and development we see the shape and movement of the whole tragedy in little. At its beginning we see Othello in complete command of himself and the island and in perfect harmony with Desdemona. By the close he is not very far from being literally insane and, though she herself is unaware of it as yet, we, the audience, are painfully conscious of the terrible fate that hangs over her. And as the play compresses 'real time' for the sake of dramatic intensity, so this scene concentrates in one long but continuous movement the extended process of Iago's domination over his master.

Act III, Scene 4

Our attention now turns to the innocent victim. After some tedious but mercifully brief fooling between Desdemona and the clown, we hear an ominous exchange between Emilia and herself about the missing handkerchief and the (to us) heavily ironic assertion that Othello is incapable of jealousy. On stage it is even possible that Emilia's question, 'Is he not jealous?' is prompted by a glimpse of Othello's demeanour as he now enters. 'O, hardness to dissemble' is double-edged for it may refer equally to Othello or Desdemona. A moist hand was reputed to be a sign of sensuality and 'liberal' carries the suggestion of being free with sexual favours, as does 'frank'. The sexual implications of 'a young and sweating devil' are obvious. Othello is already treating Desdemona as guilty of promiscuity. What is now uppermost in his mind is of course the matter of the handkerchief and he loses no time in establishing that Desdemona does not in fact have it with her. It is difficult to know how much truth to attribute to Othello's account of the history and properties of the lost handkerchief; what is clear is that the speech confers on the trifling object a symbolic, almost a mythic quality. The threefold associations of the handkerchief with marital fidelity, supernatural powers and a dying mother's gift show us that, as far as the ensuing action is concerned, 'there's magic in the web of it'. The speech also reinforces the atmosphere of larger-than-life mystery and strangeness with which Othello is surrounded.

The effect on poor Desdemona is such that she tells the first of her only two lies: 'It is not lost'. There ensues a dreadful counterpoint between husband and wife in which the words 'handkerchief' and 'Cassio' alternate like clashing weapons, with the latter winning out at the end. Desdemona, responding to Emilia's 'Is not this man jealous?', speaks truer than she knows when she says: 'Sure there's some wonder in this handkerchief:/I am most unhappy in the loss of it.'

The dialogue which takes place between Emilia and Desdemona brings out clearly the widely separate values and outlook of the speakers. Emilia sees the relationship between husband and wife exclusively in terms of appetite and possession. Women are food for men, who are only stomachs: 'and when they are full, they belch us'. It is unflattering to both sides, but the metaphor suggests that it is part of the natural order of things, to be accepted rather than rebelled against. We observe that although Emilia has nothing of the calculated ill will of her husband, her interpretation of what has happened between Othello and his wife is not very different from Iago's: Othello has sated his hunger for Desdemona and now therefore casts her out. It is a nice touch that just when Emilia begins to resemble Iago in her speech, the latter appears.

One of the multiplying ironies of the play is that the terms in which Cassio repeats his request for rehabilitation now apply as much to Desdemona:

> That ... I may again
> Exist and be a member of his love,
> Whom I, with all the office of my heart,
> Entirely honour.

The rest of the speech also foreshadows Desdemona's predicament and her ultimate decision. She speaks no more than the truth when she says 'My lord is not my lord'. Othello's identity is literally destroyed, and Iago is busy providing him with a new one as a wronged husband sworn to mortal revenge. Iago's tribute is of course spoken for his own ends, but it may be true for all that. At any rate it accords with everything we have heard and seen of Othello, and underlines, with the thrice-repeated word 'angry', the discrepancy between the martial situations in which Othello commands and the marital one which now commands him. The irony is almost unendurable when Desdemona assumes that some 'great' matter of state has made Othello over-preoccupied with some 'inferior' domestic concern, when, as we know only too well, exactly the opposite is the case. To some extent the scales fall from Desdemona's eyes here, with her rueful recognition that 'men are not gods' and that they cannot be expected to show for very long the care and devotion of bridegrooms. She blames herself for holding unreasonable expectations, but it is clear that something of her sense of the absolute and unique nature of their love has been diminished.

Emilia shows her suspicion that it may not be 'state matters' but some 'jealous toy' which has affected Othello, and in her response to Desdemona's pathetic assertion that she never gave her husband any cause for jealousy once again shows that wide-awake down-to-earth realism about human affairs of which she has already given evidence. She shows shrewd psychological insight into the self-perpetuating quality of jealousy, once again echoing Iago on the subject: 'It is a monster/Begot upon itself, born on itself.'

The brief scene between Cassio and his mistress Bianca with which the act closes serves, first, to show us that Iago's plot has succeeded, thus increasing our concern for Othello and Desdemona. In addition it presents a relationship between a man and a woman in strong contrast to the high idealism and absolute attachment of the two principal lovers at the peak of their mutual love, so fleetingly achieved and alas, already over. This is a worldly affair between an ordinary sensual man and a professional courtesan, though there appears to be more feeling on her side than his. The tone of light banter with an edge of sharpness to it is especially unrestful as our concern now is almost entirely with the fate of Othello and his bride. Bianca's parting line ''Tis very good, I must be circumstanced' faintly anticipates in a different key Desdemona's later attitude of resignation.

The spring of the tragedy is now wound up to its tightest and all we can do is be helpless witnesses as it unwinds with irresistible and utterly destructive momentum.

Act IV, Scene 1

The contrast between Othello's mental suffering and the diabolical detachment with which Iago induces and increases it is what affects us most at the beginning of the fourth act. In the earlier act, Othello's rhetorical outburst in which he likened his mental strength and resolution to 'the icy current and compulsive course' of the Pontic Sea was notably ironic in that it was spoken at the very moment when Iago was moulding him most closely towards his (Iago's) own ends. Now we see further evidence of such manipulation, with Iago boldly assuming that what is in question – whether Desdemona has been guilty of adulterous behaviour with Cassio – has in fact been proved, and that Othello is too far gone in his delusion even to utter the faintest word of protest. He can only speak of the matter in the terms Iago has offered him: whether or not an 'unauthorized kiss' and lying 'naked in bed' are consistent with guiltless behaviour. In such terms, of course, the answer seems obvious and Othello does not hesitate to pronounce it:

> *They that mean virtuously and yet do so,*
> *The devil their virtue tempts, and they tempt heaven.*

Iago now swiftly introduces the matter of the handkerchief, which assumes deadly prominence throughout this act. It has become, as Iago had planned, a symbol to Othello of his wife's honour and therefore of her love for him, that love which had led him to abandon his 'unhouséd free condition'. Iago quite literally plays devil's advocate, arguing that since the handkerchief belonged to Desdemona she had every right to do whatever she liked with it. Othello, however, is incapable now of perceiving the physical existence of the handkerchief without equating it with the guilt in which Iago has steeped it. To his demented mind the guilt has the same palpable authority as the handkerchief's existence. To his predictable response that the handkerchief is a symbol of Desdemona's honour, Iago replies in lines which, while being characteristic of his worm's eye literalism, obliquely apply to Desdemona:

> *Her honour is an essence that's not seen:*
> *They have it very oft that have it not.*
> *But for the handkerchief –*

Iago does not really need to recall the handkerchief to Othello's mind, for the Moor has certainly not forgotten it; rather, as he himself says, 'I would most gladly have forgot it!' In spite of his most determined efforts, he cannot banish it from his thoughts, which only goes to show how mistaken he was in his view that 'to be once in doubt is once to be resolved'. Throughout this act we see Othello hithering and thithering with increasing desperation between doubt and certainty and, in Bradley's fine phrase, between 'longing and loathing' for Desdemona. The metaphor of the raven haunting the plague-stricken house is apter than Othello realizes, for his mind is indeed contaminated by Iago's virulent suggestions. As he has repeatedly done before, Iago turns rapidly from the hypothetical 'What if I had said . . .' to the bland assurance that Cassio has veritably confessed his guilt. He has an unerring sense of when to give a brutally 'honest' answer and when to appear to hesitate. To Othello's anguished 'What hath he said?' he falteringly replies 'Faith, that he did – I know not what he did', and when Othello frenziedly repeats 'What? What?', Iago stalls on the single ominously ambiguous monosyllable 'Lie'. Othello must of course have his deepest fears confirmed: 'With her?', and now Iago is ready to oblige with the most vicious directness: 'With her, on her; what you will.' It is enough to cause Othello, already half-crazed with doubt and the longing for certainty, to suffer a physical collapse, preceded by an emotional breakdown signalled by a breakdown in the coherence of his language. In the chaotic jumble of phrases which he utters, the repeated motif of the 'handkerchief' can hardly escape attention, nor can the ironic inappositeness of one of the two completely lucid statements he makes: 'It is not words that shakes me thus.' For we know that it is in truth words and only words which have brought the noble and self-possessed warrior who stood erect and unafraid to plead his case before the assembled authority of the Venetian republic to be the pitiful mass of gibbering humanity we see before us now. It is a terrible tribute to the power of language to create out of 'airy nothing' (to borrow a phrase from another Shakespeare play, *A Midsummer Night's Dream*) 'the forms of things unknown'.

It may be Iago's reaction at this point, 'Work on,/My medicine, work! Thus credulous fools are caught,' that finally turns our feelings for him from grudging admiration to loathing. The lines that follow seem to anticipate with no compunction whatever the fate that lies ahead for Desdemona. We begin to realize that while Othello is in an obvious sense an outsider within the Venetian mercantile community, the real outsider is 'honest' Iago who has imposed his counterfeit image on everyone, for he seems to be an alien being to whom all human feelings, his own or others', are so much raw material to be fashioned as will or whim decides. His capacity to move instantly from feigning one state of mind to feigning another is again shown by the ease with which, as soon as he hears Cassio's approach, he utters expressions of concern for the stricken Othello. Cassio is neither more nor less gullible than Othello or any of the others in taking Iago at his word and leaving the Moor to his ensign's untender mercies. Othello's question 'Dost thou mock me?' is another reference to the tired old joke of the cuckold's horns, and Iago's elaboration of it once more shows, at least at its beginning, his tendency to regard human behaviour in 'statistical' terms:

> *There's millions now alive*
> *That nightly lie in those unproper beds*
> *Which they dare swear peculiar ...*

But he proceeds immediately, with the falsely comforting phrase 'Your case is better', to turn the knife in Othello's wound by reminding the latter of his 'true' position; at least he has the consolation of knowing the 'truth' which Iago conjures up in his tortured mind with the agonizingly vivid phrase: 'To lip a wanton in a secure couch'.

Othello's consciousness is now the helpless captive of Iago's insinuations. He has no longer any ability to see with his own eyes and judge with his own mind. Iago is therefore ready not merely to suggest what has 'happened' in the past, but actually to show Othello evidence of his wife's unfaithfulness. He is not above treating Othello with callous condescension: 'A passion most unsuiting such a man', nor, as we have seen before, of telling downright lies. His contempt for Othello makes him genuinely superior at this point, if only in a narrowly intellectual sense. *He* would not have been gulled like this. We notice how he creates in language an image of the sexually triumphant Cassio before Othello 'sees' it, so that he is certain to interpret what he sees in the light of what he has heard:

> *Do but encave yourself,*
> *And mark the fleers, the gibes, and notable scorns*
> *That dwell in every region of his face ...*

What happens to Othello's judgement in this scene exemplifies his tragic predicament almost to the very end, for his vision of reality is now constructed entirely out of materials provided by Iago. Othello clearly gives some sign of his unbearable torment, for Iago counsels him to have patience, prompting another declaration of bloody revenge, this time allied to the grotesquely inept claim that he will be 'most cunning'. (In Elizabethan and Jacobean revenge tragedy, the revenger was expected to be 'cunning' or ingenious in the execution of his purpose.)

The 'eavesdropping' scene which follows is fairly closely derived from its source, a story by Giraldo Cinthio, an Italian lawyer, which Shakespeare may have read in the original. It does not show Cassio in a very flattering light, for it is difficult to reconcile his deviousness and bragging here with the frank and courteous officer we have met earlier. Iago's knowledge of the way of the world comes out in his wry comment: 'as 'tis the strumpet's plague/To beguile many and be beguiled by one.' Othello himself is now in a position somewhat like that of Iago in the quayside scene. As the latter was there eavesdropping on Cassio and Desdemona and vowing to make mischief out of what he saw and heard, so Othello now spies on Cassio and vows mortal revenge. Cassio's innocent laughter is enough to set him on. Before our distressed eyes and ears Othello meticulously interprets every last detail of Cassio's behaviour in the light of his own frenzied jealousy: 'Look how he laughs already!', 'Now he importunes him', 'Do you triumph, Roman?' and 'They laugh that win'. It is as well for our view of Cassio that our attention, even as he speaks, is not concentrated on him but on Othello's reaction. The coarseness and ferocity of 'I see that nose of yours, but not the dog I shall throw't to' is an index of the degree to which the Iago poison has corrupted Othello.

Bianca's entry is one of those accidents which favour Iago's scheming, especially as she has the fatal handkerchief with her. Othello's resolve now seems complete: 'How shall I murder him, Iago?' is his only question. But it would be a mistake to infer from this that Othello's mind is now firmly and finally fixed on the act of revenge. What makes his situation so appalling is that he moves vertiginously between two incompatible images of Desdemona: one that of a brazen adulteress and the other that of a sweet and loving woman who freely chose him as her companion for life. Even as he strives desperately to adjust his consciousness fully to the view of his wife suggested by Iago – 'the foolish woman your wife' – the depths of his being present him an image of the other Desdemona: 'A fine woman! a fair woman! a sweet woman!' Looking back, we see now that when the Moor somewhat melodramatically banished his 'fond love' and invoked 'black vengeance', he was striving unsuccessfully to do something that went against the very grain of his soul. The stiff, artificial rhetoric of his lines, so different from the sweep and power of his characteristic mode of expression, is an indication of the extent to which his resolve is a matter of *willing*; he *wants* to feel emotions appropriate to a revenger, and that involves schooling himself to accept unconditionally the Iago view of Desdemona. But the strain is too great and nowhere does it show more poignantly than in the dizzying alternations of:

Ay, let her rot and perish, and be damned tonight, for she shall not live. No, my heart is turned to stone: I strike it, and it hurts my hand. –

O, the world hath not a sweeter creature! She might lie by an emperor's side and command him tasks.

And Iago's timely reminder, 'Nay, that's not your way', is unable to stem the violent tide:

Hang her! I do but say what she is: so delicate with her needle, an admirable musician! O, she will sing the savageness out of a bear! Of so high and plenteous wit and invention!

Iago has his work cut out to make Othello address himself to the deadly task in hand: 'But yet, the pity of it Iago! O Iago, the pity of it, Iago!'. When he wins a temporary victory, Othello's language becomes hideously like his own: 'I will chop her into messes! Cuckold me!' and there is terrible and unmistakable irony in the words with which he accepts Iago's suggestion that Desdemona should be strangled rather than poisoned: 'Good, good! The justice of it pleases. Very good!' For it is important to Othello to see himself not only as a wronged victim but, as we see later, as the instrument of an impersonal justice. But even as he resolves to kill Desdemona, he is aware of the unutterable sweetness of her actual presence and the threat it poses to his purpose: 'I'll not expostulate with her, lest her body and beauty unprovide my mind again.'

It is when Othello is in this distracted frame of mind that he and we again encounter the public, political world in the shape of Lodovico, who brings a message from Venice. In spite of ourselves we may feel a flicker of hope that some help may be forthcoming from this larger world. Some such idea seems to lie at the back of Desdemona's mind as, in her innocence, she tries to enlist Lodovico's support for Cassio and of course only makes matters worse. Each word that Desdemona utters rubs salt in Othello's wound; he cannot believe that she can be so brazen: 'Are you wise?' Even her relief at the prospect of returning home to Venice damns her in Othello's eyes, until at last he cannot endure it any longer and strikes her, calling her 'Devil!' Desdemona's very submissiveness and obedience become signs of guilt for 'trifles light as air/Are to the jealous, confirmations strong/As proofs of holy writ.'

Here we see Othello at the furthest remove from our sympathies. He is totally the creature of Iago's poisonous imagination and whatever pity we have for him now is inextricably entangled with horror and disgust at his behaviour to his wife. He seems to have accepted completely Iago's image of him as the ageing black man and lives it out. When, at Lodovico's request, he calls Desdemona back, it is only to indulge in bitter and self-lacerating mockery, playing on the sexual meaning of 'turn': 'Sir, she can turn, and turn, and yet go on,/And turn again.' The rest of the speech alternates between abusive instructions to Desdemona and distraught acknowledgement of the command from Venice to return. The thought that 'Cassio shall have my place' is evidently deeply galling, for in the very act of courteously welcoming Lodovico, it prompts the unrestrainable allusion to lecherous beasts: 'Goats and monkeys!'

Lodovico's astounded interjection vividly recalls the noble Othello he had once known, contrasting sharply with Iago's wry comment 'He is much changed', which chills us by its understatement. Iago's paltering with words, beginning with 'He is what he is', simply hides from Lodovico the speaker's own part in what the Moor has become. Almost by force of habit he resorts to the familiar technique of pretending to be unwilling to speak a truth too dreadful for the hearer's peace of mind, and the scene ends with our attention apprehensively directed towards Othello's future course of action.

This scene, like Act III, Scene 3, raises the question of how far Iago can be held responsible for Othello's plight, and what degree of responsibility we may attribute to the protagonist himself. Some critics have credited Iago with a truly 'diabolic intellect', and seen him as a villain of superhuman cunning and resource in whose grip not merely Othello but any normal human being would be powerless. Others have regarded Othello as credulous to the point of stupidity, already so insecure and inexperienced in the ways of the world where Venice and women are concerned that it needs but the merest hint from Iago to tip him irrevocably into the abyss of utter despair. Careful attention to the relevant scenes should show us that, as is often the case with critical disputes, each viewpoint points to an element that is undoubtedly present in the play and each ignores others. Othello, as we have seen, is no more credulous where Iago is concerned than anyone else in Venice. And Venetian women did have a reputation for sexual looseness. Bianca is a professional courtesan while Desdemona is a high-ranking lady, but the Bianca–Cassio relationship perhaps shows us the soldier's normal relationship with women at the time. It is also true that Othello's experience of life has hitherto been largely confined to the bivouac and the battlefield. These factors would certainly help the seeds of doubt grow and flourish in Othello's mind once they had been implanted. But it is worth stressing that Iago's timing and technique in taking advantage of them are impeccable.

Act IV, Scene 2

The bewildering alternation of Othello's feelings towards Desdemona is powerfully and painfully depicted in this scene, which begins with Othello vainly attempting to extort from Emilia some admission that her mistress and Cassio have had illicit assignations. The loyal servant steadfastly maintains her mistress's innocence, giving Othello a lesson in trust which he is too demented to learn. It is difficult to listen to Emilia without being painfully aware of how near she comes to the truth in her suspicion that some 'wretch' has poisoned Othello's mind, and how blind Othello is to what stares him in the face. To him Emilia's impassioned protestations of her mistress's innocence are only evidence that she herself is a 'simple bawd' and Desdemona 'a subtle whore'. Again, the extent to which our judgement can be coloured by suspicion and pre-conditioning is strikingly illustrated here. To her overwrought husband, Desdemona's kneeling at prayer is not evidence of piety but of hypocritical subtlety. But no sooner is she physically there before him than terms of endearment mingle with Othello's unspeakable insinuations. 'Pray chuck, come hither' he begins, but goes on immediately to treat Desdemona as if she were a prostitute and the room itself a brothel, with Emilia as bawd and doorkeeper. The emotional distance between the lovers is now at its greatest, with the innocent wife only too aware of her husband's wild anger but totally unable to account for it: 'I understand a fury in your words,/But not the words.' Othello's reply likening her to an angel who is yet about to damn herself by perjury, encapsulates the violent collision within him of incompatible feelings towards his wife. Even in his utmost anguish his love becomes a burden too great to bear: 'Ah Desdemon! Away, away, away!' Pathetic in her ignorance, she imagines Othello may be blaming her or her father for the summons recalling him to Venice. The fact that Othello makes no direct response to this shows how far he has strayed from the realm of objective events and factual likelihood. His consciousness is wholly subjugated by a nightmare vision accompanied and apparently substantiated by 'evidence' of another kind.

Most of us have probably been through some situation in which we felt that our suffering or punishment was unjust; often this feeling is accompanied by the conviction that we could have borne even greater suffering if only we had deserved it. Othello now gives the most powerful expression to this feeling in the English language. He mingles allusions to the sufferings of Job and to those of the classical figure of Tantalus, tormented by thirst yet unable to drink because the level of the water all around him sank each time he tried. The irony is of course that it is not 'heaven' that is trying him with 'affliction' but the devil Iago; even more overwhelming is the irony that his 'affliction' is totally imaginary and self-inflicted (which does not, needless to say, make it any less real to the sufferer). What Othello needs in some place of his soul is not a drop of patience but of trust. Lacking it, he conjures up for self-torment a dreadful image of himself in some condition where time is frozen into everlasting stillness and the moment of his imagined shame becomes eternal. But it is in the lines which come immediately after that we find the most poignant juxtaposition of the two views of his love that are in mortal combat within him:

> *But there where I have garnered up my heart,*
> *Where either I must live or bear no life,*
> *The fountain from the which my current runs,*
> *Or else dries up – to be discarded thence*
> *Or keep it as a cistern for foul toads*
> *To knot and gender in!*

The first three lines tell us what we must by now recognize as the exact truth about the place of his feeling for Desdemona in the totality of Othello's existence; his love is almost literally the source of his life. The image of the free-flowing fountain turning into a foetid cistern full of foul creatures in writhing copulation precisely and frighteningly embodies the change from the original Othello view of his love to the Iago view. It is Othello's heart and mind which is now the foul cistern breeding fouler imaginings, and the incomplete syntax powerfully suggests how unendurable these imaginings are. Yet the image of the 'young and rose-lipped cherubim' remains agonizingly before him in actuality. *This*, Othello thinks, is his real temptation. What self-image is he rejecting here? If he yielded to this vision of his wife, what sort of man would that make him? When Desdemona is physically there, her presence is powerful enough to dispel the degraded alternative Iago has filled him with. Even as he compares her to 'summer flies ... in the shambles,/That quicken even with blowing' the felt reality of her being prompts him to cry out:

> *O thou weed,*
> *Who art so lovely fair, and smell'st so sweet*
> *That the sense aches at thee, would thou had'st ne'er been born!*

The difference between what she physically is and what he is convinced she has been is at last too great to bear and Othello comes out with direct accusation, prompted by the sexual undertones of the word 'committed' which Desdemona uses in all innocence. By this stage our perspective on the Moor and engagement with him are radically changed. The lines in which he expresses his outrage, with phrases such as 'Heaven stops the nose at it' and 'the bawdy wind', may perhaps strike us as excessive, but only if we forget first how in all things Othello is larger than the life around him, and secondly the depth and vastness of his commitment to his love. We realize that he spoke no more than the simple truth when he said earlier that 'when I love thee not, chaos is come again'. That 'again' seems to hint at a time when, in spite of all his soldierly discipline, Othello's 'blood' (passion) ruled his 'safer guides'.

In the frenzied exchange between man and wife, the words 'strumpet' and 'whore' clamour for our attention with the raucous urgency of obscene oaths. Othello's imagination is now entirely possessed by the image of the brothel and he departs brutally flinging some coins before Emilia as a reward for her imagined 'services'. So complete is the twisted vision within him that he can actually refer to himself as a 'client' who has had his fill – 'We have done our course' – and so repugnant is the idea to him that he thinks of the 'brothel' as a chamber in hell. We may be disturbed at how easily Othello absorbs Iago's idiom; perhaps it was always lurking in the depths of his mind.

The mood changes briefly in the few lines between Emilia and Desdemona, full of tender solicitude on the servant's part and pathetic resignation on that of the mistress. Desdemona is 'half asleep', dazed with the shock of the attack on her and on the emotional reserves which she has had to call up so unexpectedly to meet it. There is a sombre note in her reference to her bed and her wedding sheets, heralding as it does the intermingling of love and death which is almost as strong in this tragedy as it is in *Antony and Cleopatra*. There is a touch of the earlier fearlessly independent Desdemona in the bitter sarcasm of her reflection: ''Tis meet I should be used so, very meet'.

It is in the highest degree ironic that Emilia, with the best motive in the world, should now call for assistance on the very person who has been responsible for the calamity. (Given the vast gap between Iago's public persona and his real nature, such irony is built into the plot, especially in the latter part of the play.) Again, Emilia is so near and yet so far from the truth:

> *I will be hanged if some eternal villain, ...*
> *Some cogging, cozening slave, to get some office,*
> *Have not devised this slander;*

I have seen this moment played with Emilia studying Iago with intent suspicion, but this seems clearly wrong. Our sense of Iago's skill in dissembling is all the keener for the realization that even his own wife does not know just what kind of creature he is. Her vigorously repeated assertion that some villain has been at work is too close for comfort for Iago, who admonishes her to 'speak within door'. But Emilia is made of sterner stuff than even her husband imagines and reminds him that someone had slandered herself and Othello to Iago. Desdemona evidently does not hear this, and Iago is at pains to silence his wife: 'You are a fool. Go to.'

Apart from the obvious irony of Desdemona pleading for help from the very man who has caused all the trouble, we cannot help being reminded, as she kneels to swear her fidelity, of the scene where Othello kneels to swear vengeance. The perception of such parallels, ironic or otherwise, is as much a part of the 'meaning' of a play as the words themselves. Both servant and master have sworn before Iago and it is terrible to realize that the peace of mind of both is now in his treacherous keeping.

That Desdemona can hardly bring herself to utter the word 'whore', let alone earn the name by her actions, is a measure of her perilous innocence. Her lines here are full of her characteristic use of absolute terms, as when she swears that she has *never* erred in thought, word or deed and that 'not the world's mass of vanity' could make her betray her marriage vows. This absoluteness, which she shares with Othello, sharply distinguishes the lovers from the hard-headed relativism of both Iago and Emilia. Iago's brusque 'I pray you be content' comes from a wholly different sphere of discourse and feeling. We can almost believe, because we so heartily wish to, that even Iago is moved by her plight as he tells her, 'Go in and weep not. All things shall be well', but we know better. The play itself, as we see, is a warning against believing what we want to merely because we want to.

Any lingering hope we may have had that Iago will mend his ways is quickly dispelled with Roderigo's entry and the ensuing conversation between them, which reminds us not only of how he has gulled Roderigo but also how he has persistently slandered Desdemona to him. Even the worm Roderigo shows signs of turning, but not surprisingly Iago is more than a match for him. He flatters Roderigo blatantly, first by telling him that so far he was only testing him and then by assuring him that he has passed the test with flying colours: 'your suspicion is not without wit and judgement'. Further flattery draws Roderigo as an accomplice into the deadly plot to murder Cassio:

> *But, Roderigo, if thou hast that in thee indeed, which I have greater*
> *reason to believe now than ever – I mean purpose, courage, and valour –*
> *this night show it.*

By dangling before the duped Roderigo's imagination the imminent prospect of sleeping with Desdemona, Iago effectively banishes from the latter's mind the reality that the action proposed is cruel and cowardly rather than courageous. Again, Iago does not scruple to use a direct lie, this one about Othello being about to leave for Mauritania unless delayed in Cyprus by some accident. His language as he alludes to the necessity of Cassio's murder typically mixes indirectness – 'the removing of Cassio' – with brutality – 'knocking out his brains'. Though Roderigo momentarily 'stand[s] amazed' at the suggestion, the fact that he is willing to hear 'further reason for this' shows the moral blindness which is as much a part of his nature as cowardice and gullibility. If Roderigo is at all typical of 'the wealthy curléd darlings of our nation', it is scarcely surprising that Desdemona had refused to marry any one of them.

Act IV, Scene 3

The short final scene of this act is full of foreboding. Othello insists on showing Lodovico round, but menacingly instructs Desdemona to dismiss her maid (a high-born maiden's personal attendant would commonly sleep in a room or passage adjacent to that of her mistress). The immense strain of preserving a façade of formal courtesy would be evident in Othello's demeanour. The rest of the scene is a dialogue, touching and at times even darkly comic, between mistress and maid in which we not only gain further insight into the close relationship between the two, but learn more of Desdemona's inner feelings and of the very different outlook on life which the two women display.

Emilia's attempt to comfort her lady – 'He looks gentler than he did' – hardly affects Desdemona. The maid seems upset at the news that she is not to be near her mistress that night. Her agitation expresses itself in her forthright exclamation 'I would you had never seen him!' but Desdemona, although she does not rebuke her maid as she might have done before the crisis, still remains loyal to her husband. We note with misgiving, however, how close to self-deception her love has come:

> *my love doth so approve him*
> *That even his stubbornness, his checks, his frowns –*
> *Prithee, unpin me – have grace and favour in them.*

In passing we also note how the interjected phrase 'prithee unpin me' reveals a clear moment of small and intimate detail which highlights the great emotional distress surrounding Desdemona. It seems that she half-realizes she is deluding herself: 'All's one. Good faith, how foolish are our minds!' Her thoughts when she is cut off from the love that is all in all to her turn as naturally and inevitably to death as Othello's turn to chaos. For both of them their mutual love is the guiding and ordering principle of their life and without it life is increasingly inconceivable. The little vignette of the maid Barbary whose lover 'proved mad/And did forsake her' poignantly foreshadows Desdemona's own fate, for Othello has indeed 'proved mad'. The song of the dying Barbary persists in Desdemona's forlorn consciousness and is yet another harbinger of her eventual doom. The song itself, sung on the stage, would both relieve and heighten the emotional tension for Desdemona and ourselves, paradoxical as this may sound. The context and words of the song, with their associations of sorrow, betrayal in love, and death, cannot fail to make us aware of Desdemona's tragic situation. Yet the very fact that it is a song which exists independently of her situation and is further 'distanced' by music and melody makes it in some sense a point of emotional rest for us and for her. The distracted reference to Lodovico which precedes it ('This Lodovico is a proper man'), with its hint of Venetian social norms, has a pathetic ring to it; the pathos is increased by the words 'He speaks well', for we are painfully aware of someone nearer to Desdemona who no longer 'speaks well' to her.

The song, then, is a way of partially distancing troubled feelings not only for us but for the singer herself. But in her case as in ours it is not wholly successful, for her own emotional state wells up unbidden before she can complete the song:

> *Let nobody blame him; his scorn I approve –*
> *Nay, that's not next.*

It is worth nothing that Desdemona, like Ophelia, can contemplate the idea of sexual misbehaviour more directly in song than in fact: 'If I court moe women, you'll couch with moe men.' Her itching eyes are one of the many signs of foreboding in the scene and in the play as a whole. A different kind of relief is provided by the discussion on adultery and the relations between husbands and wives with which the scene, and the act, closes. Desdemona's halting question to her maid leads us to believe that this is the first time she has broached the topic of unfaithful wives. Emilia's unhesitating answer shows her clear-eyed awareness of what marriage is commonly like in the real world, and the difference in their outlook is transparently clear in Desdemona's question: 'Wouldst thou do such a deed for all the world?', and Emilia's counter-question: 'Why, would not you?' The terms in which the mistress frames her question ('for all the world') are as typical of her as the forthright practicality of the response is typical of the maid. When Desdemona repeats the question in identical terms, Emilia seizes on the literal aspect of the phrase 'all the world' and contrasts it with the 'small vice' of a single act of infidelity. Desdemona cannot believe that Emilia would actually consent to be unfaithful even 'for all the world' but we should not, I think, share her confidence here. Emilia speaks with the voice of cool, unromantic reason and moral relativism for those for whom survival is the name of the game and worldly comfort not to be too easily cast aside for the sake of abstract ideals. It is not irrelevant that she belongs to a social rank in which she is wholly dependent on another's grace and favour. The repeated occurrence of 'the world' in the exchange between them compels us to take Emilia's argument seriously; she is considering the actual implications of what is to Desdemona a manner of speaking. This does not mean that we have to agree with Emilia; but it does suggest that Desdemona's admirable but naive idealism is set against a context which casts a critical light upon it. Even as the language and dramatic presence of the lovers assure us that their love is genuine, nobly idealistic and unique in this calculating community, our experience of life suggests that Emilia's no-nonsense judgements of women and men are soundly based. A good deal of the force of what she says comes from the tone which she uses. This is well brought out in the different ways in which the phrase 'the world' is used by each of them. For Desdemona it is a phrase suggesting an absolute extreme; for Emilia it is the real world in which we live, love and lie. It is her acquaintance with that world which produces the vigorous closing lines in which she puts the blame for errant wives squarely on their husbands' shoulders. 'I do think it is their husbands' faults' she declares roundly, 'If wives do fall.' It is a point of view which, though it hardly applies to Othello and Desdemona, is liable to be overlooked in all the emphasis on masculine honour being betrayed by feminine inconstancy. As Emilia sees it, men are frequently guilty of neglecting their conjugal duties or performing them elsewhere: 'pour our treasures into foreign laps'. We may contrast the characteristically physical image she uses with Desdemona's more abstract way of making the same point in her speech before the Signiory, where she referred to 'the rites for which I love him'. Secondly, men accompany this neglect with unreasonable restraints on their wives stemming from possessive jealousy. They are not above physical violence either. This, in Emilia's view, is what makes wives wander from the path of marital fidelity. Emilia's cast of mind, like her husband's, leads her to sweeping statements based on common experience rather than to an apprehension of a unique individual case. The difference between them is that Emilia can, when the moment comes, truly appreciate and passionately defend her mistress as a genuine exception to her general views on women who succumb to temptation. Her blunt warning to husbands is intended not for her mistress but for the attention of the complacent males in the audience.

Act V, Scene 1

The opening moments of Act V recall the very beginning of the play. Once again we have a scene of treachery and intrigue by night, with Iago acting as instructor in villainy to the gullible Roderigo, whose moral callousness is again shown by his comment on the proposed murder of Cassio: ' 'Tis but a man gone'. The image Iago uses in his soliloquy to describe Roderigo's present condition, that of a pimple rubbed till it is red and 'angry', is both appropriately belittling and indicative of the total domination of one man by the other. Iago's calculation plainly shows that, as far as he is concerned, there must be no survivors of the Cassio–Roderigo encounter. In part this is due to purely material and prudential considerations, namely the desirability of not having to return Roderigo's jewels and money and of preventing Othello from revealing to Cassio Iago's role in creating suspicions about him (Cassio). But the reason Iago himself gives for getting rid of Cassio betrays another aspect of his nature:

> *If Cassio do remain,*
> *He hath a daily beauty in his life*
> *That makes me ugly.*

For all his weakness in regard to drink and women, the open and honest bearing of Cassio and his apparent success in achieving promotion without recourse to influence or intrigue, constitute a direct threat to every principle of self-interest and duplicity by which Iago believes the affairs of the world to be conducted; Cassio's death is therefore as much a psychological as a practical necessity for Iago: 'No, he must die'. Perhaps something of the same compulsive force lies behind his urge to destroy Desdemona, for we surely cannot take seriously his remark that he loves her in his own way; this appears to be a remnant from Shakespeare's original Italian source.

Explanation and reflection are punctuated by a swift and violent eruption of action in the triple encounter between Roderigo, Cassio and Iago. To a marked degree the dramatic rhythm of *Othello* consists of long scenes of argument and persuasion interspersed by shorter scenes such as this one containing sharp flashes of action. The 'drinking scene', the 'handkerchief scene' and the 'brothel' scene are other examples of the latter.

Othello's delusion is now at its height, both as regards Cassio and Desdemona. Yet the effort to persuade himself of what he takes to be the hideous truth must continue unabated. Even as he calls her 'minion' and 'strumpet' he needs to exorcise her power: 'Forth of my heart those charms, thine eyes, are blotted'. The utterance expresses a wish impotent to become a fact because the wish itself does not spring from the speaker's deepest self.

The swift rhythm of the scene is maintained to the end by the rapid 'cutting' from one group to another. The technique is almost cinematic. First we have Iago and Roderigo, then Roderigo and Cassio with a brief interruption by Iago; next attention moves to Othello himself and from him to the entry of Lodovico and Gratiano and their discovery of the wounded Cassio. Iago's re-entry focuses our attention on him and leads to the stabbing of Roderigo. No sooner have we taken this in than a further centre of interest is established with the entrance of Bianca, which Iago promptly turns to his advantage by turning suspicion for the wounding of Cassio on her. The action is so rapid and the confusion so great that it may take some effort to keep firmly in mind the one incontrovertible fact that Shakespeare has taken such pains to present: that the entire scene as it is played out before our eyes has been 'directed' by Iago from first to last. His successful attempt to make Bianca appear guilty is a minor example of his usual technique of 'slanting' evidence by framing it within a particular viewpoint:

> *I pray you look upon her.*
> *Do you see, gentlemen? Nay, guiltiness will speak*
> *Though tongues were out of use.*

It is a technique that reminds us once again, as we almost fall victim to it, of one of the play's major themes: the precarious foundations on which judgements are often based.

The effortless efficiency with which Iago has taken command not only of the immediate situation but also of the 'official' version of what has happened extorts our admiration even though we are repelled by its calculating callousness. Emilia becomes the innocent instrument whereby Iago's interpretation of events is expressed, and her reaction, 'Alas, good gentleman! Alas, good Cassio' is just what Iago would like to be the response of all concerned. Iago is, characteristically, not averse to some sanctimonious moralizing: 'This is the fruit of whoring'. We know only too well that this 'fruit' is from a wholly different poison-tree, but the double standard taken for granted by both Iago and Emilia is worth noting. Bianca is castigated by both as a 'strumpet' but Cassio who, if there is to be any question of guilt, is at least as guilty to say the least, becomes 'poor Cassio'. Both social rank and gender are involved in this distinction, Emilia being outraged by Bianca's claim to be as 'honest' (sexually pure) as herself. We may remember an earlier occasion when another woman had made the same claim and not been believed. The dire consequences of that disbelief are to provide the calamitous climax of the tragedy, now almost upon us. Our interest is now engaged almost entirely with the principal pair, and the relentless selfcentredness with which Iago views all that has happened and is about to happen is very much at odds with our own viewpoint:

> *This is the night*
> *That either makes me or foredoes me quite.*

Act V, Scene 2

In performance, we would be strongly aware of the contrast in rhythm, atmosphere and emotional tone between the bustling, confused and rapid action of the earlier scene and the troubled stillness of this one. Three times in as many lines Othello repeats the phrase 'It is the cause'. It is almost as if the words cast a hypnotic spell over him, as if they were a charm which Othello needs to bear with him in order to perform the deed to which he has now dedicated himself. But what do the words mean? And why does Othello not want to name 'it'?

The word 'cause' had several different senses in Elizabethan English, most of which survive today, though they are not always clearly distinguished in modern usage. Two immediately relevant and related meanings are, first, the reason which prompts a particular action, and secondly, the object or end towards which an action is directed. In these senses, the 'cause' of Othello's present desperate situation is Desdemona's imagined infidelity, and the 'cause' to which his action is directed is the restoration of justice and the moral order breached by her supposed transgression. Elizabethan usage also admitted a straightforward legal sense of 'cause' meaning an accusation brought against someone in court. This sense is psychologically very important to Othello, because one of the things that support him in his crisis is the conviction that he is an agent of impersonal justice, a judge carrying out without favour his appointed task of meting out due punishment to the offender. Precisely in proportion to the involvement of his personal feelings, indeed his whole being, in Desdemona and his image of her, Othello needs to preserve an image of himself as a detached and impartial judge. For this purpose, the legal implications of 'cause' are vital. Finally, there is the sense of 'cause' which occurs in the modern phrase 'a good cause', the idea of something which it is morally right to strive for. This is clearly related to the legal sense but is wider in scope, and it elevates Othello's sense of himself from the narrowly legal to the moral or spiritual plane. It will be seen, then, that the precise sense and significance of the phrase Othello utters like a mantra vary according to which sense of 'cause' is uppermost in his (and our) mind. I am far from suggesting that we must suppose Othello to be consciously playing on the different senses of the word; he is much too distracted to be indulging in word games. But Elizabethan dramatists, and Shakespeare most of all, were very consciously interested in the several meanings of a single word (it was part of a general interest in the English language denoting an emergent nationalism), and rarely missed an opportunity to bring them into play, sometimes dragging them in with scant regard to propriety or relevance. Othello's obsessive repetition of the phrase 'It is the cause' indicates that at *some* level of his consciousness he senses the power and resonance of the key word.

That he cannot bring himself to 'name' the cause is also highly significant. As we have seen, the 'fact' of Desdemona's unfaithfulness is one that Othello cannot bring himself to face directly. He can, under Iago's evil spell, temporarily infect himself with the latter's corrupt and corrupting imagery, but this process is constantly interfered with by the memory and the living presence of his wife. In this last agonizing scene, therefore, Othello can only fulfil his dreadful task by keeping its monstrous actuality at a distance from him, and by dramatizing both himself and his victim in ways which will bolster his resolve. His refusal or inability to 'name' the 'cause' truly is one part of the process. Another is his determination not to 'shed her blood'. As a mercenary soldier

Othello has doubtless shed much blood in the 'causes' of others. Yet outside the battlefield blood has long been a symbol of murder and guilt and Othello is resolved to avoid both. It is as if, by killing Desdemona and yet leaving her unscarred and unblemished, he can achieve his aim as self-appointed justicer, and at the same time preserve the image of the Desdemona he knew and loved undefiled for ever. As he gazes on the sleeping figure before him, the radiant whiteness of her skin contrasts in his mind with the violent red of the blood he cannot bring himself to spill, but in his words the living Desdemona almost becomes the carved effigy on her own tomb:

> *Yet I'll not shed her blood,*
> *Nor scar that whiter skin of hers than snow,*
> *And smooth as monumental alabaster.*

As before, he almost falls under the spell of the living presence and its beauty and must recall himself to his self-appointed task by an effort of will: 'Yet she must die, else she'll betray more men'. Earlier Othello had asserted how little he would have cared if the entire army had enjoyed Desdemona, so long as he himself had remained ignorant. His present utterance falls on our ears as unconvincingly as the earlier one. Yet it is not the pathetic falsity of the statement that here impresses us so much as the willed insistence on himself as the instrument of justice. And here we come across a crucial confusion or rather conflation in Othello's mind as he recreates himself as the symbolic figure of Justice. For justice to be carried out it is necessary to have both an impartial judge and an efficient, conscientious and independent executor (or executioner). In most civilized societies the roles are carefully separated. Othello sees himself now as judge, now as executioner. To make matters more tragically complicated, he also unites within himself the roles of plaintiff and victim. Thus he has symbolically internalized the entire process of law, and, furthermore, elevated that process into a moral rather than a merely legal one. Perhaps there is an indirect allusion here to a secular state which takes insufficient account of the fact that Justice needs to go hand in hand with Mercy. It is not surprising that nothing, not his own experience of Desdemona, nor memories of their courtship, nor the plain evidence of his senses and the testimony of Emilia, nor, finally, the anguished pleas of Desdemona herself, can make any inroads into the massive strength of this many-layered self-image.

It is perhaps clear now that Othello's emotional state makes it *necessary* for him to symbolize himself, his action and his intended victim. He literally cannot bear to think of her as she is, so he turns to the symbolism of light and the rose tree. Perhaps this virginal vision of her had always been more potent in his consciousness than that of the real, living woman with her own nature and needs. He trembles on the brink of the realization that the deed he now contemplates is awesome in its irreversibility. Repentance is still in his thoughts, as if in some forlorn corner of his mind the conviction of Desdemona's innocence still lingers, stricken but alive. The palpable beauty before him is haunting in its power: 'Thou cunning'st pattern of excelling nature', though the word 'cunning'st' carries with it not only the usual Elizabethan sense of 'exquisitely created' but the modern meaning of 'artful' or 'devious' as well. The allusion to Promethean fire recalls the fire from heaven which gave man life and reminds us how literally Othello's life depends on the fire of Desdemona's ardent love. Even the ultimate action of the kiss needs to be symbolized and 'purified' in Othello's imagination by the metaphor of the rose on the tree. The physical action once more all but succeeds in making the executioner stay his weapon. The interfusion of love and death reaches its highest intensity in the lines:

> *Be thus when thou art dead, and I will kill thee,*
> *And love thee after.*

Perhaps, as has been suggested above, he can cope with the ideal, immobile image more easily than with the real woman. At any rate it is imperative that he should retain the image of himself as the minister of heavenly justice, and that the cruel and senseless act he is about to commit be seen by him as an act of love:

> *I must weep,*
> *But they are cruel tears: this sorrow's heavenly —*
> *It strikes where it doth love.*

When Desdemona wakes, even those who are familiar with the tragedy will hardly be able to repress a faint and forlorn hope that even at this latest minute of the hour she will be reprieved from a cruel, unnecessary and totally unwarranted fate. In the last fatal encounter between husband and wife, this hope keeps flickering within us until it is finally and brutally extinguished. When we see it on the stage we are shockingly aware of this brutality as Othello smothers Desdemona, and the contrast between Othello's conception of his act and what we see affects us powerfully. Othello is determined now to see his intended action as justice rather than revenge, and is careful to preserve all the formalities as far as the condemned 'prisoner' is concerned. He solicitously inquires whether she has said her prayers, reminding her of the need for full and frank confession in order to maintain her soul's purity:

> *I would not kill thy unprepared spirit:*
> *No – heaven forfend! – I would not kill thy soul.*

Othello may have come from an exotic pagan background, but he is a Christian convert and Christian ideas are very important, at least to his conscious mind. In his famous stage portrayal of the Moor some twenty years ago, Laurence Olivier wore an enormous golden cross round his neck which he tore off savagely when he vowed to take revenge. This may have been intended to suggest that Othello's Christianity was barely skin-deep, a matter of conscious will. If so, it may have overstated the case, for Othello returns to Christian ideas not only in his intellect but in his imagination in his last moments.

Our attention at this point is evenly distributed between the avenger and his victim. Desdemona's reaction is a compound of fear, bewilderment and desperation and she herself draws attention to Othello's behaviour with her references to 'when your eyes roll so' and 'why gnaw you so your nether lip?'. In the polygonal Jacobean theatre, with its vast audience and poor sightlines, such descriptions of a character's bearing would help quicken the imagination of those spectators who could not see his face in clear detail.

Dr Johnson remarked in his essay on this play on 'the slowness of Desdemona to suspect that she is suspected'. This is perhaps a bit unfair to Desdemona for, being completely innocent, she has no grounds whatsoever to suspect that her husband believes her to have committed adultery with Cassio or anyone else. Her persistent pleading on the latter's behalf to Othello may strike us as tactless, but only because, from our superior viewpoint on the action, we know how it affects Othello. In reality it is the clearest proof of her innocence as well as the immediate cause of her doom. By the time she has elicited from Othello the one external 'fact' on which he bases his conviction of her guilt (the handkerchief), it is already far too late for her to convince him otherwise. Othello himself, with unwitting irony, testifies to the degree to which he is no longer amenable to rational judgement on the matter:

> *Therefore confess thee freely of thy sin;*
> *For to deny each article with oath*
> *Cannot remove nor choke the strong conception*
> *That I do groan withal.*

We have seen the Moor literally 'groaning' with 'the strong conception' that Iago has filled him with. If not even Desdemona's oath can dispel it, this is partly because *no* evidence of a material kind can destroy suspicion that an intimate relationship has been betrayed. Apart from the difficulty of proving a negative (that is, that Desdemona has *not* been unfaithful), the damage is done with the mere raising of the doubt. The disastrous irony is that Othello, while being immune to the subjective 'evidence' of Desdemona's guiltlessness (such as her own sworn word and her love for him), is fully persuaded by the wrong kind of evidence, namely the mere material fact of the handkerchief in Cassio's hand. 'Send for the man and ask him' pleads Desdemona desperately, but in vain. Othello's mind is now completely closed as he warns her to 'Take heed of perjury'. When she swears as plainly and passionately as she can that she has never betrayed his love, Othello is all the more convinced of her guilt. The possibility that she is innocent can no longer be given full admission into his mind for at least two powerful reasons. The first is that Iago is 'honest' and Othello cannot conceive of a world where such devastating malice can exist. Secondly, succumbing to Iago's vision of an unfaithful wife and a cuckolded husband has cost the Moor so much anguish and self-division that he cannot admit the possibility that it was all totally unfounded and unnecessary; he *needs* to believe in the reality of his torment, and that presupposes the reality of the cause of that torment. From his present standpoint Desdemona, by denying the (literally) incontrovertible 'fact' of her guilt, is degrading the exalted quality of his act of justice, for in addition to his other self-created roles Othello sees himself as a priest about to perform an act of ritual sacrifice and purification:

> *O perjured woman! Thou dost stone my heart,*
> *And mak'st me call what I intend to do*
> *A murder, which I thought a sacrifice.*
> *I saw the handkerchief.*

The bare and undoubtedly true statement in the last line has become in Othello's frantic mind equivalent to another, totally false proposition, that Desdemona gave Cassio the handkerchief as a token of their illicit passion. Her repeated plea that Cassio be sent for falls on deaf ears, for 'he hath confessed'. Irony piles up on irony as we reflect with distress that Othello, who is incapable of believing the woman who has sacrificed everything for him, so readily swallows the lies of the man who has set out to destroy him. Even the fact that Cassio will (as Othello believes) have no opportunity to deny his guilt becomes proof of that guilt. Against this kind of imperviousness no attack is of any avail. Othello's stony resistance here to appeal and argument is typical of that callous disregard of others except as instruments of his own appetites and aspirations which is the trade mark of Iago. Desdemona's despairing cry 'My fear interprets' shows her growing and belated awareness of the truth, but also describes in brief the whole process by which Othello has come to delude himself: it is because of the fear and insecurity brought about by discrepancies of age, race and upbringing that Othello falls, under Iago's guidance, to 'interpret' or rather misinterpret reality so tragically.

In the original Italian story the counterpart of Othello kills Desdemona by causing the four-poster bed on which she is sleeping to fall on her. Apart from the practical problems of having this enacted on the stage, Shakespeare had good reason to trust the dramatic instinct or experience which led him to devise an ending which is both more powerful and more appropriate. Othello must kill his victim with his own hands, as the priest must carve the sacrificial offering himself. With his terse 'It is too late' it seems that our last hope for Desdemona's survival has gone. But Emilia's call prompts Othello to look at the motionless figure and realize that she is not yet quite dead. The Moor touches a low point in our sympathies as he considers how to escape discovery even in the act of making sure his victim is dead. There seems to be something empty in the grandiloquent rhetoric with which he contemplates a world without Desdemona:

> *O, insupportable! O heavy hour!*
> *Methinks it should be now a huge eclipse*
> *Of sun and moon, and that th'affrighted globe*
> *Should yawn at alteration.*

In many tragedies, the death of an important figure is accompanied by reference to natural portents: 'the heavens themselves blaze forth the death of princes'. These lines may recall Cleopatra's lament over Antony's death or Macbeth's after the discovery of Duncan's murder, but we feel them to be less appropriate on the lips of one who has committed murder by strangling a woman. Perhaps Othello is expressing here what he *will* feel but is afraid to feel. His resort to lies – 'I had forgot thee' – and what he imagines to be cunning – 'Let me the curtains draw' – does nothing to enhance our idea of him here. His response to the news of Roderigo's death and Cassio's escape is again Iago-like in its attention to others only as instruments in one's own plans and desires. The third climax in this final scene (the first being the awakening of Desdemona and the second her strangling by Othello) comes with her brief recovery and final relapse.

That her last words should be an acceptance of blame for what has happened is wholly characteristic of Desdemona, to whom unquestioning obedience and loyalty to her husband have been part of the meaning of marriage. If we recall her words before the Signiory, we may see in them now a sense sadly different from any the speaker then intended:

> *That I did love the Moor to live with him,*
> *My downright violence and storm of fortunes*
> *May trumpet to the world.*

If we are determined to see a moral in her death, let it be one less obtuse and more imaginatively generous than Rymer's self-satisfied stupidity: 'This may be a caution to all Maidens of Quality how, without their Parents consent, they run away with Blackamoors.'

We may reflect that part of the vision of tragedy is of a world where innocence can be dangerous and may incur guilt, though the play encourages us to avoid the extremes of regarding Desdemona as wholly innocent (and therefore a moral nonentity) or entirely culpable; we must never minimize either Othello's share in her fate or Iago's deep complicity in bringing it about.

For a moment it appears that Othello has descended to the shabbiness of using Desdemona's dying words to provide an alibi for himself, but he only uses them as further evidence of her moral duplicity in being a liar to the last. Perhaps it is the need to establish Desdemona's guilt in some other court than that of his own mind which leads Othello to confess to Emilia. Our dramatic attention is once more divided between the speakers. Emilia's immediate reaction to Othello's confession, 'O, the more angel she,/And you the blacker devil', is typical of her and a timely reminder of the 'ordinary' attitude to Desdemona. We should note that Emilia does not for a moment consider the possibility that her mistress could have been in the slightest degree false. As far as she is concerned, her experiential knowledge of Desdemona utterly precludes such a possibility, as it should have done for Othello. The only question for her is how such a monstrous falsehood could have entered Othello's mind in the first place. For the Moor there now comes, too late, the beginnings of a painful lesson in seeing reality as it is. In the rapid interchange between them we hear a single word, ominous in its reference, repeated so often that even Othello becomes impatient: 'What needs this iterance, woman? I say thy husband.' But for Emilia, the repetition of 'husband' registers the paralysing shock with which her mind takes in the appalling knowledge that 'honest' Iago, the man whom everybody trusts and who has shared

71

her life all these years, was the knowing agent of this wanton destruction. She needs to have it hammered home to her consciousness, and once it is finally lodged there, her reaction is every bit as passionate, direct and unerring as we have come to expect of her:

> *If he say so, may his pernicious soul*
> *Rot half a grain a day! He lies to th'heart.*
> *She was too fond of her most filthy bargain.*

In that last line we may hear perhaps what Emilia had all along thought of her mistress's marriage but was too prudent and loyal to utter. Now she is convinced that her worst fears were well founded and her feeling that the Moor was in every respect unworthy of her mistress comes out in her outspoken attack on Othello, which has an emotionally releasing effect on the audience as it expresses a good part of what we feel:

> *O gull! O dolt!*
> *As ignorant as dirt! Thou hast done a deed –*
> *I care not for thy sword – I'll make thee known,*
> *Though I lost twenty lives. Help! Help, ho! Help!*
> *The Moor hath killed my mistress! Murder! Murder!*

In contrast to Othello's persistent exaltation of his deed of destruction, here is the plain, simple and clear voice of the real world, crying real murder. The degree to which Emilia's straightforward language here reflects our own feelings is the measure of the emotional distance that now separates us from Othello.

The killing of Desdemona is now not only a stage in Othello's moral decline but an event in the public, external world. As Othello had conceived it, the act had been single and simple, emotionally as well as spiritually and even aesthetically satisfying. In his tormented mind it had shone with a lucid purity and distinctness as a ceremony of justice and ritual sacrifice. But with the words of Emilia and the entrance of Montano, Gratiano, Iago and others, the word 'murder' begins to be heard repeatedly, to remind us of the real nature of the deed. To the end Emilia clings to the notion that Iago cannot be guilty of the slander which Othello has attributed to him. Iago's reply to her desperate plea, 'Disprove this villain, if thou be'st a man', is characteristically evasive yet it contains a dreadful truth:

> *I told him what I thought, and told no more*
> *Than what he found himself was apt and true.*

It is indeed precisely true that Iago told Othello what he thought (or pretended or wanted to think) rather than what was actually the case; and it is just as true that Othello found a truth which did not ever exist. Emilia, however, is not the woman to be put off by evasions and Iago has to answer her direct question 'But did you ever tell him she was false?' with an unequivocal affirmative. The floodgates of Emilia's grief and wrath are now open and she no longer doubts who the real villain is nor cares about the consequences to herself of revealing the enormity she has discovered. We are now aware of yet another structural irony in the play, namely the contrast between the marital relationship of Othello and Desdemona on the one hand and of Iago and Emilia on the other. Desdemona is the wife falsely suspected while Iago is the husband whose falseness goes unsuspected till the very end. There is a grim similarity in the deaths of both women, for both are wantonly killed by their husbands to preserve the latters' 'security' or 'honour'. Both women are also emblems of loyalty and true devotion even unto death, Desdemona steadfastly defending her husband, Emilia her mistress. Mention should also be made here of the only other woman in the play, the courtesan Bianca, who, for all the coldness and hard-headedness associated with her profession, remains loyal to her lover in the face of great personal danger. In their different ways, therefore, the three women provide instances of loyalty, courage and steadfastness sadly lacking in most of the play's male characters.

With Desdemona dead, Emilia now becomes the fearless and outspoken champion of her mistress's innocence. There is a hint of what is to come in her answer to Iago's command that she go home: 'Perchance, Iago, I will ne'er go home', while Othello's inarticulate cry expresses both his sense of loss and a growing bewilderment in the face of which he desperately strives to cling to his conviction that 'she was foul!' The news of Brabantio's death only increases our feeling of the sheer waste involved in Desdemona's. Nor is Othello permitted to rest secure in his own evaluation of what he has done. The real world, in the shape of Emilia, has more to teach him. The fatal handkerchief, so momentous an item in his distorted imagination, is now restored to its true dimensions in the clear and courageous words which cost Emilia her life. Her outraged question to Othello, 'what should such a fool/Do with so good a wife?' is harsh enough, but it also echoes what Othello has tried so hard to suppress: his growing awareness that he is indeed unworthy, not on racial or social but on purely human grounds, to be Desdemona's husband. The smothering of Desdemona can now be seen as Othello's attempt to suppress that part of himself which contains this painful knowledge. Of course Othello is guilty of murder, but to an extent he also commits self-murder.

The realization, when it comes, of what he has actually done destroys Othello's image of himself as righteous avenger. It also all but destroys his belief in a moral universe: 'Are there no stones in heaven/But what serve for thunder?' he cries out, as Iago kills his wife who, like her mistress, dies for the truth. Her dying words, 'O, lay me by my mistress' side', remind us of this affinity. Montano's brusque instruction to Gratiano to kill Othello if he tries to escape gives us a glimpse of how the latter appears to the objective view, as one who has committed a capital offence. The final moments of the play alternate between these two views of the tragic killing: the anguished inward vision of the killer himself; and the troubled but severe judgement of the public world, represented by Montano, Gratiano and Lodovico.

Othello's vision of himself touches its nadir in his self-pitying yet strangely self-neglectful reflection:

> *I am not valiant neither,*
> *But every puny whipster gets my sword.*
> *But why should honour outlive honesty?*
> *Let it go all.*

These lines gather into themselves a good deal of the meaning and emotional impact of the tragedy at this point. A sword will very shortly figure prominently, both as symbol and physical object. The key words 'honour' and 'honesty' have been charged with enormous significance by their earlier uses. Othello has always prided himself on being a man of honour both on and off the battlefield and has been recognized as such by all, including Iago. But another sense of honour, that of a man's reputation, especially as it can be affected by his wife's misbehaviour, is equally present to Othello here. Othello has betrayed one idea of honour by behaving to Desdemona as if *she* had betrayed another. 'Honesty' of course contains the sexual as well as the more general meaning of the word. At one level, the former sense may suggest that Othello is still thinking of Desdemona's imagined lapse, but it is he himself who has tainted the idea of sexual fidelity by mistrusting his wife, and therefore been 'dishonest' in the wider sense. The realization of this double betrayal leads to the despairing resignation of 'Let it go all'.

On the stage Emilia's last words, especially her echo of Desdemona's willow song, often have a heart-stopping poignancy. They momentarily give us a perspective on events different from that of Othello's tormented conscience or the objective judgement of the representatives of the Venetian state. It is the standpoint of the innocent victim, whom tragedy, the least sentimental of genres, often shows being swept to destruction in the wake of the hero's fall. If we cannot assent to Emilia's judgement of Othello as the 'cruel Moor' we can certainly sympathize with the feelings that lead her to make it.

The stabbing and eventual death of Emilia seem to have turned Othello's thoughts inward and compelled him to re-evaluate his own motives and actions, especially the last fatal one. We no longer find in him the rhetorical power which was the verbal sign of the man's inner integrity and self-confidence; speech is now both difficult and painful to him. In performance his silences would be heavy with emotional resonance. With his revelation that he has another weapon, 'a sword of Spain, the ice-brook's temper', he begins the slow journey towards the rebuilding of a more satisfying image of himself, one that will not evade or excuse his undoubted guilt, but will set it in a more comprehensive and comprehensible context. This is the only sense in which Othello can be called an egoist, that the construction of his image of himself can be more important to him than reality itself. In a way his sword becomes a sort of visual equivalent of the 'Othello music' which he recovers in the play's final moments. When he declares 'Uncle, I must come forth' (recalling his 'I must be found' at the very beginning), it is not merely leaving the room in which he is being held that Othello refers to, but also the necessity that he must 'come forth' in the sense of openly declaring himself and his position. He begins with a piece of characteristic self-dramatization; 'Behold, I have a weapon'. But we should bear in mind that self-dramatization is not always a sign of self-delusion or complacency. It may be, as here, an emotional necessity which is precisely true to the actual situation. Othello now has the advantage over those who attempted to restrain him, and the sword is a token both of his superiority and of his former soldierly-presence. The contrast between this and his present condition leads him to speak words which have real pathos but also a touch of self-pity, rather like a similar moment in *King Lear* when the old crazed king recalls:

> *I have seen the day, with my good biting falchion*
> *I would have made them skip; I am old now,*
> *And these same crosses spoil me.*

Similarly Othello remembers that

> *I have seen the day*
> *That with this little arm and this good sword,*
> *I have made my way through more impediments*
> *Than twenty times your stop . . .*

and the thought leads him to see himself as the victim of an inescapable destiny – 'Who can control his fate?' – which is the last resort but one of the tragic hero confronted with his own error. When he asks those about him not to be afraid he may be externalizing his own fear about what is to come, though the question 'Do you go back dismayed?' seems to be a disguised stage direction giving us a clue to the reaction of those on stage. The metaphor of Othello's life as a voyage, first expressed in his speech to the Senate and actualized in the journey to Cyprus, now reaches its haunting climax in:

> *Here is my journey's end, here is my butt*
> *And very sea-mark of my utmost sail*

where sound and sense are both rich with the eloquence we have learned to associate with the heroic Othello. The contrasting image which follows immediately, of Othello as utterly feeble and defenceless, marks the speaker's awareness of how his existence has diminished with the death of Desdemona: 'where should Othello go?' As he approaches the murdered corpse he tries to see her too as a victim of blind fate rather than his own tragic folly – 'O ill-starred wench!' (an allusion to her name) – but is still overwhelmingly aware of her physical presence: 'This look of thine will hurl my soul from heaven'. At last he is able to recognize her innocence, associating it with the fact of her death: 'Cold, cold, my girl,/Even like thy chastity', and the recognition immediately provokes a devastating awareness of the scale of his criminal folly and with it a sense of the punishment he deserves. The masochistic yearning for torture cannot be disentangled from its opposite, the desire for self-extinction:

> *Whip me, ye devils,*
> *From the possession of this heavenly sight!*
> *Blow me about in winds! Roast me in sulphur!*
> *Wash me in steep-down gulfs of liquid fire!*

At last Othello is able to recognize what his consciousness has been refusing to admit ever since he committed the dreadful deed: the reality and finality of Desdemona's death. Fittingly, he voices it in the barest and simplest of words – 'O Desdemon! Dead Desdemon! Dead!' – and even this naked utterance collapses into the wordless anguish of the repeated 'O! O!' No dramatist has exploited as powerfully as Shakespeare the eloquence that lies at the very limits of language, most notably in *King Lear* but on a smaller scale at the end of *Othello* too.

The final moments bring together all the principal characters involved in the tragedy. There are at least three main centres of interest: the innocent victims, Desdemona and to a lesser degree Emilia and Cassio, the largely unwitting agent of destruction Othello, and the arch-villain, now a prisoner, Iago. Surrounding these central figures are the representatives of civic authority led by Lodovico and Montano. The stage presents a picture of a kind of trial scene, as it has done at key points throughout the play. Lodovico's question 'Where is this rash and most unfortunate man?' takes some note of Othello's own version of himself but is also literally true, as is Othello's answer, tinged though it is with a degree of self-dramatization: 'That's he that was Othello: here I am.' To the extent that Othello's life has been inextricably intertwined with his love for Desdemona, he ceases to exist with the destruction of that love; killing Desdemona was tantamount, in more ways than one, to destroying himself.

The confrontation between Othello and Iago is full of dramatic power and our interest is heightened by the second disarming of Othello. It is difficult to judge just how Iago speaks the line 'I bleed, sir; but not killed'. Is he triumphant, taunting his victim? resigned to his fate? detached and neutral? making a last desperate play for sympathy? However he says it we are bound to feel a twinge of irrational horror at the underlying suggestion that Iago, being almost the devil himself in his callousness and delight in deliberate evil-doing, is indestructible. Iago carries whatever mystery he embodies to the end, for his last words are resolutely opaque:

> *Demand me nothing; what you know, you know:*
> *From this time forth I never will speak word.*

But we must not, for all that, make too much of a mystery of Iago, for we know a good deal more about him than anyone on stage. Indeed we know something which is hidden from Iago himself, namely the deep-seated insecurity which leads him to strike at and dominate whatever or whoever he imagines may prove a threat to him. Given his initial assumption that the truly successful man is he who forestalls betrayal by betraying whoever crosses his path, Iago is driven by the necessity of constantly proving this; and the need for an audience's approval finally leads him to over-reach himself.

Gratiano's grim remark 'Torments will ope your lips' gives a chilling glimpse of an age when the torturing of prisoners was taken for granted (as it still is in many parts of the world). There follows a more or less clumsy piece of tying up of loose ends involving the always convenient letter (or even two) found in the pocket of a dead man, explaining all. Perhaps the reason we do not find this device as objectionable as we otherwise might is that *we* do not need Roderigo's letters, as we already know the truth. In any case our interest now is in things other than details of plot. The mystery of the handkerchief is finally revealed to Othello, as is the real cause of the brawl that led to Cassio's dismissal. To complete the resolution of the plot we have Roderigo's death-bed confession of complicity in Iago's plot to oust Cassio.

Nothing now remains, as far as external action is concerned, but for Lodovico, the appointed representative of Venetian authority, to take charge of the prisoners and nominate a governor for Cyprus. Yet we would be deeply disturbed by a conclusion in which Iago and Othello shared the same fate, and our expectations of tragic form lead us to anticipate Othello's end. Another reason for this is that, as pointed out earlier, in an important sense Othello has already destroyed himself, so that his physical self-destruction is only the outward recognition of what has already taken place.

But if Othello's death is inevitable, the manner of his dying is crucially significant. He begins on a note of deliberate understatement: 'I have done the state some service and they know't', reminding his listeners that he is entitled to be heard. As with many great tragic heroes, his final concern is that the world shall know the truth: 'Speak of me as I am'. He then makes his own last attempt to do just this, seeing himself as the victim of an all-consuming and therefore imprudent love. To the end he considers himself to have been 'one, not easily jealous but, being wrought,/Perplexed in the extreme'.

But can we agree with this view of Othello? That he was deliberately 'wrought' by Iago is indisputable, as is the tragic consequence of such diabolical manipulation. But was Othello 'not easily jealous'? Jealousy can signify either suspicion or possessiveness (apart from enviousness, which is not relevant here). There is little evidence that Othello's attitude towards his bride contained an unusual proportion of either of these elements before Iago set to work upon him. He makes no effort to ensure that Desdemona goes to Cyprus in the same ship, and we remember that Cassio acted as go-between during their courtship. Before Iago's vile innuendo had affected his judgement, he was capable of being just and rational on the subject of marital jealousy:

> *'Tis not to make me jealous*
> *To say my wife is fair, feeds well, loves company,*
> *Is free of speech, sings, plays and dances well:*
> *Where virtue is, these are more virtuous.*

It is true that Othello was *made* jealous, but it took a great deal of Iago's cunning and experience as well as his carefully built up reputation for honesty to achieve this, to say nothing of outright falsehood. Othello's downfall was certainly not brought about by a mere piece of 'dramatic mechanism' as one critic would have it. On the other hand, we have seen that underlying Othello's great love were certain misgivings about his age, colour and background which, *once brought to the surface* by Iago's cunning insinuations, were enough to 'unprovide' his mind. Thus we are brought to understand that Othello's tragedy is *his* in the sense that his nature and history are essential to it, but also that it needed the conscious, careful and persistent interference of Iago to bring it about.

Othello's comparison of himself to a savage who unthinkingly throws away a precious jewel affirms his sense of the value of what he has lost through his own ignorant thoughtlessness. (The word 'Indian' occurs in the Quarto text, while the Folio has 'Judaean' suggesting betrayal rather than ignorance; the Folio reading may be due to nothing more than a compositor's error.)

Othello's death, like his whole career, has a romantic and heroic quality about it, though 'romantic' is not used here in any belittling sense. In his mind's eye he sees himself in the here and now, weeping (as the original actor probably did on stage), but the tears are in some way healing or 'med'cinable'. A necessary prelude to his death, however, is the recovery of his former idea of himself. In a sense, although Desdemona is dead, her pristine image has been restored to Othello by the revelation of Iago's treachery. Now he needs to restore his own sense of self so that he may be imaginatively reunited with her, as Cleopatra in her dying moments is reunited with Antony. He does this by recalling a moment which epitomizes both his professional and personal self. Professionally he acts as the loyal servant of the Venetian state, defending her against her enemies and traducers. Personally he behaves like a Christian hero displaying both courage and faith. But in his final act he becomes both the Christian hero and the heathen villain whom he destroys, his former mistrustful and destructive self. Perhaps the Christian Othello needs this double view of himself in order to overcome the Christian ban against suicide (no Christian hero commits suicide in a Shakespeare play). Thus he becomes both killer and victim, acknowledging his responsibility for Desdemona's death and avenging it at the same time. His very last words, 'Killing myself, to die upon a kiss', combine the motifs of death and sexual fulfilment which we have already encountered at the opening of the scene. (To 'die' was a term used to denote sexual climax in Elizabethan English.) As he falls dying upon the bed where Desdemona lies, the stage offers us a visual image to which Lodovico draws attention in words addressed to Iago but full of meaning to us as well: 'Look on the tragic loading of this bed.' It is indeed a scene that 'poisons sight' and the words 'Let it be hid' are a stage direction to an actor to cover the corpses, marking the final 'official' recognition of the tragedy before other needful business is attended to. For it is one of the characteristics of Shakespearean tragedy that however catastrophic the tragic hero's fate may be and however great the destruction he wreaks, we are never allowed to forget that there is a larger world elsewhere and that life, however slowly and painfully, must go on.

Part Two: Some topics of interest

We have followed the course of the tragedy in as much detail as space permits, as it unfolds before us on stage or page. The information we have accumulated in doing so should help us to arrive at an informed opinion on a number of questions raised by the tragedy. Many of these have been touched on briefly in connection with particular scenes and passages, where a critical comment (on the character of Desdemona, for instance, or the motivation of Iago) is made in the context of evidence offered in support of it. This seems to be the best method not only of increasing our knowledge of the play but of preventing general questions from breaking free of their firm grounding in the play and floating off into vague and airy abstraction. But while our view of character, situation and motive is gradually forming as we become acquainted with the developing drama, it is only at the end that we are in possession of *all* the evidence necessary for a full and balanced response. The remainder of this study will therefore be concerned with developing some topics central to *Othello* which have been touched on earlier in specific contexts. The discussion in this final section will be mainly general, mostly omitting particular examples, partly for reasons of space but mainly in order to encourage readers to recall for themselves supporting or refuting evidence for what is said.

Othello as tragic hero

In an obvious and trivial sense there is no question but that Othello is a tragic hero, since *Othello* is a tragedy and its hero or principal figure is Othello. But there are important differences between Othello and other Shakespearean tragic protagonists, such as Hamlet, Macbeth and Lear. To begin with, Othello, though descended from kings, is not himself a prince or king in the society of the play, but only a mercenary. Since Ibsen and Arthur Miller's *Death of a Salesman* we have got used to the idea of the tragedy of the common man, but in Shakespeare's day and as far back as Aristotle's, tragedy usually had a monarch at its centre (though a homespun variety of domestic tragedy was beginning to emerge on the Elizabethan stage). This was not so much for reasons of snobbery as because in most earlier societies, since they were organized in rigid and closely linked hierarchies, the death of a king had profound consequences for the life of the society over which he ruled. As Rosencrantz puts it in *Hamlet*:

> *The cease of majesty*
> *Dies not alone, but like a gulf doth draw*
> *What's near it with it; it is a massy wheel,*
> *Fix'd on the summit of the highest mount,*
> *To whose huge spokes ten thousand lesser things*
> *Are mortis'd and adjoined; which, when it falls,*
> *Each small annexment, petty consequence,*
> *Attends the boisterous ruin. Never alone*
> *Did the king sigh, but with a general groan.*   (I.3.15)

This brings us to one of the key features of the tragic hero's fate, namely that it changes the lives of those about him. In the case of *Othello*, Venetian society is purged of a canker through realization of the true nature of 'honest Iago', but the fact that Othello is a paid servant, albeit a highly respected one, rather than the ruler of the state diminishes the range of impact of his tragic fate (the secular mercantile society of Venice is also rather less hierarchically organized than traditional monarchic societies). Othello's tragic career affects only a few individuals within his immediate circle. This is one of the reasons why *Othello* has sometimes been called the most domestic of Shakespeare's tragedies. While matters of state certainly figure in the play, especially at the beginning, they are marginal to it and often serve as metaphors for the play's central themes of judgement, misjudgement and the uses and abuses of evidence; the central interest of the tragedy is firmly personal and marital.

The tragic hero, like Hamlet or Lear, is gradually or suddenly afflicted with a vision of evil and corruption at the very foundations of his world. In the case of *Hamlet* and *Lear*, this vision is true insofar as evil does exist where the protagonists see it; in *Macbeth* the hero sees evil in the villain, who is himself. But Othello sees evil where it does not exist, in Desdemona, and only too late in Iago who truly embodies it. This lack of perception, while it may make Othello more sympathetic as a fallible human being, perhaps diminishes his tragic stature.

The tragic hero suffers greatly, but as a result of his suffering he is able to see more clearly into himself and into the nature of the world about him. Othello, when he has shed his delusion, understands that the world contains both the innocence of Desdemona and the wickedness of Iago.

But almost to the end he seems to be imperfectly aware of his own responsibility for the catastrophe. It is only at the very end that he achieves some degree of imaginative understanding of those elements in his nature which contribute to the tragedy. This realization on Othello's part is vital, for it contributes to the sense of responsibility for his own fate which is an important element in our idea of the tragic hero. Othello's tendency to self-dramatization never deserts him, but, as has been suggested, this is not necessarily a weakness; it may be a spectacular example of heroic ideals being an essential part of the imaginative reality which the hero inhabits.

Thus, in spite of the crucial role played by Iago in his downfall, Othello has the dignity, freedom of choice and self-responsibility that define the tragic hero. It is somewhat paradoxical that though *Othello* is the most intimate and small-scale of Shakespearean tragedies, Othello himself is a more than life-size hero, one who in his language, appearance and bearing carries with him more than a suggestion of a richer and more spacious world than the one in which he finds himself. In the most general terms, his tragedy is rooted in his transition from one world to another.

What makes Iago tick?

Coleridge's famous remark about 'the motive-hunting of a motiveless malignity' does point to one aspect of Iago's nature. His need for an audience is so great that he is constantly presenting us with a choice of motives, as unconcerned over which of them is really genuine as a conjuror appears to be over which card we may pick from the fanned-out pack. But Coleridge's comment is misleading in its suggestion that Iago has no motives whatsoever. It is rather that his motives, or his motivation, differ very often from what he makes them out to be, and are even hidden from himself. A deep-rooted contempt for fellow human beings, based on the insecurity of a self-made man, is a constant element in his make-up, while at a more obvious level his acquisitiveness should not be overlooked. His carefully built up image as the honest, practical, no-nonsense soldier who speaks as he finds and has neither time nor taste for intellectual sophistication is the result of intelligence, psychological skill and patient planning. He is much more than a mere device to trigger off Othello's egoism. It might be said that he becomes, as the plot grows in complexity, something like a cog in his own devilish machinery, except that he retains almost to the end his capacity for thinking on his feet.

Consideration of Iago's nature should not, however, be confined to his manipulation of Othello, but should take into account his dealings with all the other characters, including his wife. In doing this, it will be helpful to try and distinguish between what Iago wishes various other characters to believe about him, what he wants the audience to believe, and what he betrays about himself unwittingly. To Roderigo, he presents himself as a crafty and worldly-wise accomplice with an axe of his own to grind. To Cassio he is first the jovial boon companion, then the concerned fellow soldier. To Desdemona he is the licensed misogynist and later her lord's troubled underling. To his own wife he shows a brusque contempt which he doubtless intends to suggest an underlying affection. In all this Iago is certainly a calculating villain, but it would be a mistake to emphasize the element of cold intellect in his character at the expense of the furious passion of self-regard which animates him throughout.

The women in the play

In a great play, which *Othello* undoubtedly is, characters are not conceived merely as separate individuals but also in relation to each other and, equally important, for the light they throw on the concerns of the play in question. For the purposes of discussion it is inevitable, however, that at certain points each character should be considered separately. Thus the three women in the play, Desdemona, Emilia and Bianca, share certain similarities and display certain differences which illuminate the play as a whole. They also deserve and demand consideration as individuals in their own right.

Desdemona has too often been seen either simply as the purely innocent victim of malice, misunderstanding or accident or as somehow responsible, through some 'flaw' in her nature, for the terrible fate that befalls her. Neither of these extreme views does justice to the complexity of Shakespeare's portrayal and the play as a whole, as already suggested, warns us against such simplistic 'absolute' judgements on human beings. On our first acquaintance with her we are impressed by Desdemona's candour and courage and the resoluteness of her attachment to Othello. She has been capable of rejecting prospective suitors chosen for her by others, and of defending her own choice to an irate and uncomprehending father before the assembled authority of the state. She is also capable of a certain hard-headed practicality (we recall that she was responsible for the running of a large household) in her acknowledgement of the consequences of her choice. Together with this realism, however, is a romantic vision of her husband which remains tragically inflexible to the end. It needs to be added immediately that Desdemona's romantic view of Othello is to a large extent validated by the reality of the man himself. Othello *is* a romantic figure, if the word has any meaning at all. He is exotic, noble, courageous and generous in word and deed. Nevertheless, Desdemona's view of her husband remains static and this contributes to the tragedy. Desdemona has committed herself to a certain image of Othello, and her psychological and even physical survival depends on her maintaining this commitment. She tries, but only half-heartedly, to modify this image in the light of the plain evidence of Othello's changed behaviour, but literally cannot bring herself to do it. Rather, she attributes the change in Othello to anything – affairs of state, anxiety about being recalled to Venice, resentment over her father's attitude – except to her husband's altered perception of herself. This accounts for her tactless persistence as well as her inability to recognize that she is suspected. To recognize this would be to alter her idea of Othello and that she cannot do. She goes on believing that nothing is wrong with their relationship while Othello becomes increasingly convinced that the opposite is the case. Thus the reaction of each only aggravates the other, until the public humiliation of being struck in the face compels Desdemona to see that, for whatever reason, Othello's view of *her* has changed. With this recognition, a strange indifference to the future comes over her, contrasting strongly with her vivacity and boldness, even her gaiety in the earlier part of the play. She almost begins to resemble the description of her given by Brabantio to the Senate at the beginning. Her protests when Othello is about to murder her strike us as quiescent rather than desperate. Without the love for which she has staked all, life makes no sense to her, and when she is 'bereft' of that love she more than half accedes to the taking of her life. Though Othello has betrayed their love, she remains steadfastly loyal to him and it to the very end.

Like Desdemona, Emilia and Bianca are seen, the former partly the latter entirely, in their relations with men. The contrast between Desdemona and her maidservant is evident in their language and attitude, but certain affinities, though perhaps less obvious, are equally noteworthy. Emilia is of course a far more experienced woman of the world, probably older than her mistress. Her years of marriage to Iago seem to have sharpened an already unillusioned view of men and women. But we need not assume, because she frankly expresses the view that husbands who are unfaithful deserve to have their wives follow suit, that this view is based on her own experience or practice. Everything we know about her suggests that she has been a loyal and caring wife to Iago and that she remains so until his real nature becomes apparent. In this she resembles her mistress, though the limits of her tolerance are narrower than Desdemona's. Emilia's view of her mistress's marriage has naturally always been more detached than Desdemona's, but it has never been close to Iago's confident cynicism. She seems to have recognized instinctively the gap between her relativistic outlook and Desdemona's idealism. When the depth and extent of her husband's treachery is revealed, Emilia's reaction is unflinching and far more positive than Desdemona's. With her dying words she expresses her absolute faith in her mistress's virtue, and her devotion embodies a faith and loyalty which surpasses her common-sense realism.

Though in some editions of *Othello* the list of characters describes Bianca as a courtesan, we do not see her in the play in a professional capacity. There she appears as a devoted and warm-hearted lover of Cassio who is prepared for her love's sake to undergo rebuff and humiliation. Her jealousy over the handkerchief is no less real than Othello's, though it does not lead to the same murderous vindictiveness. The play makes it clear that both kinds of jealousy are totally without any basis in reality. Like Desdemona, Bianca is capable of being hurt just because her love is genuine. One of the play's leading ideas is that our need of others, while it makes us human, also makes us deeply vulnerable. In this respect Bianca is more like Desdemona than any other character in the play, and if we find it difficult to think of the heroine of a great tragedy as being in any way like an acknowledged harlot, it is because our vision is not as wide or as generous as Shakespeare's.

Race and colour

Shakespeare wrote two plays in which the question of racial difference plays an important part and he set them both in Venice. This is not surprising when we consider the degree to which its incessant and far-flung commercial activity had made the republic a kind of cultural melting pot. It is obvious that Othello's tragedy would not have occurred in the way it did if the Moor had not been of a different race and colour from most of those in the society about him. But the sense in which Othello's race and colour contributed to his downfall needs to be carefully distinguished from vague attributions of racial prejudice. There are those in

Venice who are racially bigoted, but Venice as a whole does not appear to be a racist society, at least where Othello is concerned. The general esteem in which he is held, Brabantio's earlier regard and affection for him and the Duke's remark on hearing his story, show that this 'extravagant and wheeling stranger/Of here and everywhere' has earned himself a respected position in Venetian society. But he is respected for his professional experience and capability and for those personal attributes of authority, self-discipline and judgement that go with them. Few in Venice, Othello himself included, can see the man within the soldier. Indeed, it may be misleading to put it this way, implying that the Moor's 'essential' nature was independent of his history and experience. Brabantio's radically changed attitude when confronted with Othello as a son-in-law is revealing, perhaps even representative (in spite of the Duke's aside). As long as he looks at Othello as a professional soldier, Brabantio has nothing but admiration and affection for him. But forced to consider him in a more intimate relationship, he is trapped in the cultural stereotype of the black man as ugly, cruel, lustful and dangerous, near cousin to the devil himself. Brabantio, perhaps like the rest of Venice, is prepared to make an exception of Othello (just as prejudiced people today are often prepared to admire individual black people for their distinguished achievements 'in spite of' their colour), but only in his soldierly capacity. Outside of that he is simply a black man, with all that the stereotype implies, and only witchcraft could account for a beautiful, intelligent and high-born maiden becoming enamoured of him.

Brabantio speaks wiser than he knows. There *is* a kind of witchcraft in the way Desdemona has come under the Moor's spell, for which the fatal handkerchief briefly acts as a symbol. The enchantment seems to be compounded of two elements. First, there is the mystery and romance of his heroic and adventurous past: 'She loved me for the dangers I had passed'. We may, as mentioned earlier, have our doubts about the strength and durability of this kind of attraction as the basis for a secure marriage. But there is also the magic spell of a unique and absolute commitment based on a subjective and intensely felt perception of the individuality of each person by the other. This uniqueness of perception and commitment represents a way of judging and feeling in total contrast to the generalizing habit of mind constantly displayed by Iago. Nor does the play in any way suggest that the latter is a superior or more reliable attitude where people are concerned. From this point of view, Othello's colour may stand as a visual symbol of the uniqueness of Desdemona's choice, which is not to deny the reality of that choice but to define it.

Othello is a black man, but his blackness does not raise problems about integration and racial harmony; it simply acts as a reminder to us of both the strangeness and the individual quality of Desdemona's choice. That choice, like many decisive choices in people's lives, is made from the depths of one's own being and not based on statistical considerations of probable success or failure. In fact, it very often involves a conscious or unconscious exempting of oneself from the category of statistics. Faced with a really momentous choice, we cease to regard ourselves as representative instances and look inward to our own nature and needs. This is what both Othello and Desdemona have done, and as long as they both keep faith with that momentous act of choice they are invulnerable; Othello's colour can even become, for Desdemona, the occasion for a mild joke (III.4,30–31). But once Iago has succeeded in converting Othello into his own 'statistical' way of thinking, the tragedy is inevitable. Othello then begins to see Desdemona not as the unique and irreplaceable human being who had eyes and chose him, but as a Venetian girl, super-subtle and headstrong, who has gone her own way once in defiance of male authority, and may do so again. And worse still, he begins to see himself not as the unique object of Desdemona's choice but as Iago 'programmes' him to see himself – black, old, uncivilized and so on. Why he should accept Iago's stereotypes of Desdemona and himself is a question that goes to the very roots of Othello's identity.

Thus Othello's colour is dramatically important as a symbol of his own uniqueness and the uniqueness of Desdemona's choice, but it is only when Othello begins to think of himself as a 'typical' black man (and his bride as a 'typical' Venetian girl) that the seeds of tragedy are sown.

Othello and the modern audience

Purely as a theatrical experience, *Othello* is as rich and satisfying as only the greatest drama can be. But like all great imaginative work, it speaks to us of our own world, even though it came out of a very different one. I hope the commentary has made it clear that many of the issues the play raises are relevant, with very slight modification, to our own time. Among the major ones are: The way in which stereotypes are created and come to be accepted (Othello's, Iago's, Desdemona's); women's perception of their own role and men's perception of women; the bases on which people make judgements of others, and the extent to which these are influenced by their own needs and interests; and the nature and limits of one's own responsibility for what happens to oneself. But we should always be fully alert to the concrete situation in which such matters are presented. It is only by patient and continuous attention to the way these and other questions are given flesh and blood through poetic language and dramatic action that we can succeed in relating the play to our own lives without oversimplifying it or diminishing or distorting its impact.

Text and performance

The first performance of *Othello* of which we have documentary evidence took place at Court in the autumn of 1604. There was also a performance in 1610 at Oxford. Ever since Shakespeare's celebrated fellow-actor Richard Burbage played the title role, *Othello* has been one of the most popular of Shakespeare's plays, and almost every important tragic actor has played the role at least once, while several actresses made their name as Desdemona. In 1669 Margaret Hughes as Desdemona was probably the first woman to appear on the English professional stage.

It is interesting to note that on several occasions the parts of Othello and Iago have been played on alternate nights by two actors in a single production. Among the great actors who have played the title role are David Garrick and Spranger Barry (to Charles Macklin's Iago) in the eighteenth century, John Philip Kemble, Edmund Kean and Henry Irving in the nineteenth, and in our own century Donald Wolfit, Paul Robeson and Laurence Olivier (with Frank Finlay as a memorably plausible Iago). Notable Desdemonas have included Susannah Cibber, Mrs Siddons, Ellen Terry, Peggy Ashcroft and Maggie Smith.

The popularity of the play is not difficult to understand for it has all the qualities of dramatic tension and contrast, exotic character and a strongly emotional central situation which make for success in performance. Its powerful dramatic rhythm consists of an alternation between scenes of swift and violent action and longer scenes of argument and reflection. In its language, the opulent poetry of Othello and Iago's spare and wiry prose serves not only to characterize their respective worlds, but also to enhance the sense of mighty opposites heading towards inevitable collision. The two central characters, Othello and Iago, are richly portrayed in themselves as well as in their relationship to each other and Desdemona, as has been pointed out, is far more than a passive victim.

Finally it may be reiterated that whatever problems the so-called double time' of the play may raise in the study, in performance it is barely noticed. It is true that although the action of the play covers just over twenty-four hours, the plot demands, among other things, a long-standing adulterous relationship between Cassio and Desdemona (or rather, the possibility of one) for which no time is allowed. But in an adequate production the pace of events as well as the heightened emotional states of Othello and Desdemona capture the audience's attention and interest to such a degree that the question 'When did all this intrigue take place?' simply never arises.

The play was first published in 1622, six years after Shakespeare's death, in a Quarto edition (Q). In the following year it was included in the First Folio edition of Shakespeare's works edited by his fellow actors John Hemmings and Henry Condell. The F text is based on a copy of Q corrected by comparison with the playhouse prompt-book. Each text has lines not found in the other and a modern edition is based on both. Quotations in this study have been taken from the New Penguin Shakespeare text edited by Kenneth Muir.

Suggestions for Further Reading

Like all Shakespeare's plays, *Othello* has been exhaustively written about. The following is a drastically selective reading list.

A. C. Bradley's fine essay in *Shakespearean Tragedy* (1904) gives a widely influential view of the play which is attacked in an equally influential essay by F. R. Leavis, 'Diabolic Intellect and the Noble Hero', reprinted in *The Common Pursuit* (1953; Peregrine Books 1962). Wilson Knight's essay on the play in *The Wheel of Fire* (1930) is also well worth reading and thinking about, as is John Bayley's in *The Characters of Love* (1960). There is a characteristically stimulating essay on the use of 'honest' in the play in William Empson's *The Structure of Complex Words* (1951).

The dramatic structure of the play is given detailed examination in Harley Granville Barker's Preface (1930) and its theatrical interpretation in Marvin Rosenberg's *The Masks of Othello* (1961). Two full-length studies of the play are Robert Heilman's *Magic in the Web* (1956) and *Othello as Tragedy* by Jane Adamson (1980).

A fuller reading list is given in the New Penguin Shakespeare, edited by Kenneth Muir.

FOR THE BEST IN PAPERBACKS, LOOK FOR THE

In every corner of the world, on every subject under the sun, Penguin represents quality and variety – the very best in publishing today.

For complete information about books available from Penguin – including Pelicans, Puffins, Peregrines and Penguin Classics – and how to order them, write to us at the appropriate address below. Please note that for copyright reasons the selection of books varies from country to country.

In the United Kingdom: Please write to *Dept E.P., Penguin Books Ltd, Harmondsworth, Middlesex, UB7 0DA*

In the United States: Please write to *Dept BA, Penguin, 299 Murray Hill Parkway, East Rutherford, New Jersey 07073*

In Canada: Please write to *Penguin Books Canada Ltd, 2801 John Street, Markham, Ontario L3R 1B4*

In Australia: Please write to the *Marketing Department, Penguin Books Australia Ltd, P.O. Box 257, Ringwood, Victoria 3134*

In New Zealand: Please write to the *Marketing Department, Penguin Books (NZ) Ltd, Private Bag, Takapuna, Auckland 9*

In India: Please write to *Penguin Overseas Ltd, 706 Eros Apartments, 56 Nehru Place, New Delhi, 110019*

In Holland: Please write to *Penguin Books Nederland B.V., Postbus 195, NL–1380AD Weesp, Netherlands*

In Germany: Please write to *Penguin Books Ltd, Friedrichstrasse 10–12, D–6000 Frankfurt Main 1, Federal Republic of Germany*

In Spain: Please write to *Longman Penguin España, Calle San Nicolas 15, E–28013 Madrid, Spain*

In France: Please write to *Penguin Books Ltd, 39 Rue de Montmorency, F-75003, Paris, France*

In Japan: Please write to *Longman Penguin Japan Co Ltd, Yamaguchi Building, 2–12–9 Kanda Jimbocho, Chiyoda-Ku, Tokyo 101, Japan*

NEW PENGUIN SHAKESPEARE

General Editor: T. J. B. Spencer

FOR THE BEST IN PAPERBACKS, LOOK FOR THE 🐧

PENGUIN CLASSICS

John Aubrey	**Brief Lives**
Francis Bacon	**The Essays**
James Boswell	**The Life of Johnson**
Sir Thomas Browne	**The Major Works**
John Bunyan	**The Pilgrim's Progress**
Edmund Burke	**Reflections on the Revolution in France**
Thomas de Quincey	**Confessions of an English Opium Eater**
	Recollections of the Lakes and the Lake Poets
Daniel Defoe	**A Journal of the Plague Year**
	Moll Flanders
	Robinson Crusoe
	Roxana
	A Tour Through the Whole Island of Great Britain
Henry Fielding	**Jonathan Wild**
	Joseph Andrews
	The History of Tom Jones
Oliver Goldsmith	**The Vicar of Wakefield**
William Hazlitt	**Selected Writings**
Thomas Hobbes	**Leviathan**
Samuel Johnson/ James Boswell	**A Journey to the Western Islands of Scotland/The Journal of a Tour to the Hebrides**
Charles Lamb	**Selected Prose**
Samuel Richardson	**Clarissa**
	Pamela
Adam Smith	**The Wealth of Nations**
Tobias Smollet	**Humphry Clinker**
Richard Steele and Joseph Addison	Selections from the **Tatler** and the **Spectator**
Laurence Sterne	**The Life and Opinions of Tristram Shandy, Gentleman**
	A Sentimental Journey Through France and Italy
Jonathan Swift	**Gulliver's Travels**
Dorothy and William Wordsworth	**Home at Grasmere**

FOR THE

PENGUIN MASTERSTUDIES

This comprehensive list, designed for advanced level and first-year under-graduate studies, includes:

SUBJECTS
Applied Mathematics
Biology
Drama: Text into Performance
Geography
Pure Mathematics

LITERATURE
Absalom and Achitophel
Barchester Towers
Dr Faustus
Eugenie Grandet
Gulliver's Travels
Joseph Andrews
The Mill on the Floss
A Passage to India
Persuasion *and* Emma
Portrait of a Lady
Tender in the Night
Vanity Fair

CHAUCER
The Knight's Tale
The Pardoner's Tale
The Prologue to the Canterbury Tales
A Chaucer Handbook

SHAKESPEARE
Hamlet
Measure for Measure
Much Ado About Nothing
A Shakespeare Handbook